Poverty and Growth
in a South China County

Poverty and Growth in a South China County

Anxi, Fujian, 1949-1992

Thomas P. Lyons

East Asia Program
Cornell University
Ithaca, New York 14853

This book is number 72 in the Cornell East Asia Series. The
series is published by the Cornell University East Asia
Program and is not affiliated with Cornell University Press.
We are a small, non-profit press, publishing reasonably-priced
books on a wide variety of scholarly topics relating to East
Asia as a service to the academic community and the general
public. We accept standing orders which may be cancelled at
any time and which provide for automatic billing and shipping
of each title in the series upon publication.

If after review by internal and external readers a manuscript is
accepted for publication, it is published on the basis of camera-
ready copy provided by the volume author. Each author is thus
responsible for any necessary copy-editing and for manuscript
formatting. Submission inquiries should be addressed to
Editorial Board, East Asia Program, Cornell University,
Ithaca, New York 14853-7601.

To Chun-Mei

Contents

List of Tables and Figures

Tables

Figures

Preface

Fifteen months ago, I set out to write a short paper for a conference on South China, to be convened at Cornell in October 1993. I had in mind a paper weaving together two strands of research that I had begun to explore in earlier work. One of these two strands concerns the persistence of poverty in China, and China's attempts during the 1980s to come to grips with the poverty problem. The second concerns the playing out of national and provincial policies at the local level—the role of local decision-makers, the policy instruments used, the latitude for genuinely "local" development strategy. A case study of a single locale seemed appropriate. I chose Anxi simply because it had the distinction of ranking last, among all the counties of Fujian province, in many measures of development.

My short paper grew into this short book, as I assembled bits of evidence that might shed light on Anxi's experience and explored the resulting mosaic. I hope that this fairly detailed account of one county's recent economic history will provide a basis for comparison with development paths elsewhere and will buttress larger interpretations that, to date, have lacked firm grounding in data.

I thank the East Asia Program at Cornell, for research support that allowed me to travel to Fujian and Hong Kong; Jean Hung, for helping me gather relevant materials; Bruce Stone, for generously sharing unpublished agricultural data; and Victor Nee, William Parish, Bruce Reynolds, and Su Sijin, for providing helpful comments on an earlier version of Chapter 3. I owe special debts of gratitude to Peter McClelland and Henry Wan, Jr., for encouragement at times when it was sorely needed. Finally, I wish to thank friends in Fujian for their patience and for invaluable assistance—though, in deference to their wishes, I refrain from naming them here.

February 1994

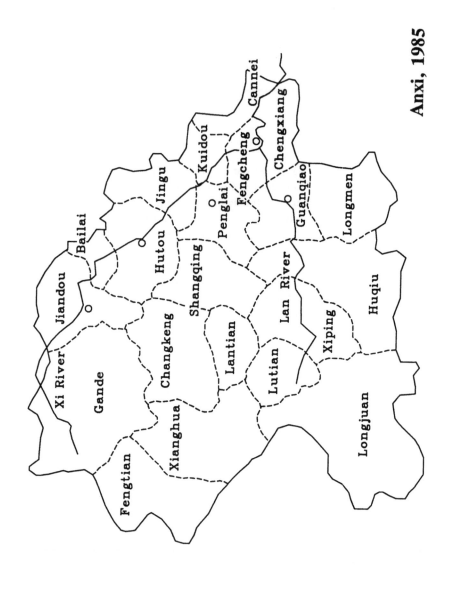

Anxi, 1985

1
Introduction

Since the late 1970s, China's southeastern coastal provinces have grown more rapidly than any other region in the world—a "South China miracle," hailed in both the popular press and in scholarly analyses. For South China as a whole, this miracle constitutes a remarkable departure from the lackluster performance of the preceding twenty-five years. But to what extent has it reached into the region's poorest corners—into counties that, prior to the late 1970s, suffered severe deprivation? How have such counties changed? Do the post-Mao changes in such counties shed new light on the causes of their poverty during the Maoist era?

While there is now a massive literature on economic reform and economic development in China, almost all of this literature deals with national policies and national trends. The literature focusing on the playing out of larger policies at the regional and local levels remains quite small.[1] Very little is known about the spatial pattern of development during the post-Mao era, the processes by which growth has spread, or the dynamics of economic "miracles," in South China or elsewhere. And, of course, it remains unclear to what extent the Chinese experience has relevance for poor locales in other countries.

This book examines the experience of one South China county—Anxi county, in Fujian province. In the late 1970s and early 1980s, Anxi was famous for its poverty: the number of poverty-stricken households in Anxi far exceeded that in any other county in Fujian, and rural income per capita in Anxi was the lowest in the province. But, as Chinese observers point out, Anxi is in some respects a case of poverty amidst plenty.[2] It is also famous for superlative teas and fruits, for rich mineral resources, and—historically, if less so today—for lush mountain forests.

While Anxi is a special case in terms of the extent of poverty, it is quite representative in other important respects. It was, for example,

1

neither a model of Maoist rectitude prior to 1979 nor a hotbed of reformism thereafter. Anxi is of interest because, in this respect, it is *not* special. And, although Anxi is located in a coastal province, the county itself is off the beaten path: it has no harbors and (until the mid 1980s) no railroad, and it is not adjacent to any city. Hence, insofar as China's reopening is concerned, Anxi may be a precursor for the many areas even farther removed, by geography and policy, from coastal "windows" open to the modern world.

The central questions taken up in this book concern (1) Anxi's development efforts, in terms of local policies affecting the mobilization and deployment of labor, the allocation of investable resources, and the modernization of agricultural and industrial technology; (2) the changing structure of Anxi's economy, as reflected in the sectoral composition of employment and output; and (3) the standard of living in Anxi, and the major sources of improvement therein. These questions are addressed primarily by appeal to the sizable body of county-level data now available in national compendia and in provincial yearbooks, journals, and news-papers.[3] At some points, unpublished data are also used—but mainly to provide additional detail rather than to introduce propositions that cannot be tested with data from public sources.

An examination of any single county's economy is of necessity an inquiry into the larger context of central and provincial decision-making, as well as national and provincial events and trends. Decisions of higher levels may directly affect the local pattern of economic activity—when, for example, the province decides to build a factory in the county. More generally, decisions of higher levels shape the opportunity sets of the county government, by delimiting the sorts of policies that the county can legitimately consider, and of individual agents, by defining "rules of the game" governing their economic activities. Some such higher-level decisions, while not aimed at Anxi in particular, have proved to be of special significance to the county, due to its endowment, its overseas connections, or pure chance; other decisions have explicitly targeted Anxi, either individually or as a member of a group (such as the group of designated poverty counties).[4]

Throughout Chapters 2 through 4, developments in Anxi are placed in the context of larger institutional constraints, national and provincial policies, and recurrent mobilization campaigns imposed from outside the county itself. Chapter 2 examines the county's development efforts between the early 1950s and early 1980s and the results of these efforts, concluding with an interpretation of Anxi's development pattern under Maoism. Chapters 3 and 4 then turn to the post-Mao era and the impact of "reform and reopening" upon Anxi's economy. Chapter 3 focuses in particular upon the responses of the local government and of farmers and businessmen to opportunities created by the new policies; Chapter 4 focuses upon changes in the structure of the local economy and the implications of these changes for the welfare of county residents.

Two general conclusions merit mention at the outset. First, Maoism, as a poverty-oriented development strategy, was not successful in Anxi. External constraints characteristic of Maoism—such as barriers to internal and international trade—severely distorted the county's development prior to the early 1980s and contributed to the emergence of "chronic" poverty.[5] Second, although relative disparities may widen as a result of post-Mao policy changes, Anxi and, certainly, other poor counties are benefiting rapidly and very substantially from the new opportunities these changes are creating. Interregional *inequality* may well be a legitimate concern; however, to date the post-Mao changes have not caused *immiserization* in Anxi (through "backwash effects" from growth elsewhere) to any appreciable extent. Rather, the "spread" or "trickle-down" of growth is clearly predominant.

The remainder of this chapter briefly describes Anxi's natural endowment and the county's relations with the larger Fujian economy.

Geography.[6]   Anxi is located at the western edge of Jinjiang prefecture (renamed Quanzhou municipality in 1984).[7] Originally a part of Nanan county, Anxi became a separate county in 955 AD and has existed as a county ever since. With a land area of roughly 3000 square kilometers, Anxi is comparable in size to the state of Rhode Island and is considerably larger than Hong Kong or Singapore.

In terms of climate and topography, Anxi is broadly representative of China's southeastern interior (Table 1.1). The county's climate is monsoonal, with rainfall concentrated in late spring and summer, and with hot summers and mild winters (except in the highest elevations).[8] Most of Anxi's land lies at elevations of over 500 meters, with terrain ranging from rolling hills to rugged mountains. Anxi is criss-crossed by winding streams, most of which empty into the Xi and the Lan; the bulk of the county's lowland area (only 14.8 percent of the total area) lies along these two rivers. Soils are generally of the red types common in the southeast; these soils tend to be acidic, clayey, erosive, and deficient in plant nutrients—and, hence, are problematic to manage.[9]

In recent times, roughly half of Anxi has been covered by forests, mainly of pines; the forested area, however, declined quite sharply between the 1950s and the 1980s. Only about 10 percent of the total land area is

Table 1.1. Natural Resources and Population, Anxi County

Location	
longitude	117°36'-118°17'E
latitude	24°50'-25°26'N
Land	
total land area	2963 km²
	(4,440,000 mu)
>800 meters above sea level	24.6%
500-800 meters	38.4%
200-500 meters	22.2%
<200 meters	14.8%
cultivated area	
1952	435,900 mu
1957	476,500 mu
1980	411,300 mu
1992	393,000 mu
Surface Water	
rivers and streams, total length	>1000 km.
Xi system, main stream and 6 tributaries	319 km.
Jiulong system, 3 tributaries	155 km.
usable hydroelectric potential	180,000 kw.
large reservoirs, 1981[a]	12,600,000 m³
Forests	
forest cover (share of total land area)	
1957	60%
1985	40%
timber reserves	
1957	1,772,000 m³
1985	1,312,000 m³

Table 1.1, continued

Mineral Reserves

iron ore	87,315,000 tons
coal	12,147,000 tons
limestone	96,000,000 tons
graphite	300,000 tons
manganese, lead, zinc, kaoline, pyrophylite	commercially significant amounts

Climate

average temperature	
January	10.8° C
July	28.3° C
frost-free days	260 (west) - 350 (east)
annual precipitation	1500-2000 mm.

Population

1829	254,800
1941	356,400
1957	390,300
1980	728,600
1992	943,900

Note: For detail on cultivated area and population, see the Appendix.

a. Includes only the 46 reservoirs having capacities of at least 100,000 m³.

Sources. Fujian sheng cehui ju, following p. 36; Zhang and Lu, pp. 569-71, 575; Minnan85, p. 120; FJJJNJ87, pp. 633-35; FJJJ, November 1988, pp. 29-30; Chen Jingsheng, pp. 179-80; FJTJNJ93, pp. 473, 495; Tables A1 and A6 (in the Appendix).

arable.   And Anxi suffers serious erosion, due to heavy rains and the attendant swelling of rapid mountain streams, the erosive properties of its soils, and deforestation.

Local resources and transport costs vary considerably within Anxi. Indeed, the county is conventionally viewed as consisting of two distinct regions, known as "outer" and "inner" Anxi. These are separated by a line running from the town of Hutou in the north to eastern Huqiu in the south.

Outer Anxi—roughly, the eastern one-third of the county—includes the edge of the Quanzhou coastal plain along the lower Xi and Lan Rivers; much of the region, however, is hill country. Outer Anxi falls within the "Lowland Agricultural Zone of Eastern Fujian," one of six land-use zones identified in recent provincial surveys. Within agriculture, outer Anxi produces mainly field crops (rice, sweet potatoes, sugar cane, peanuts, and local specialties), fruits, and pigs and poultry. With up to 350 frost-free days per year and with an average of over 1500 mm. of rainfall annually, outer Anxi is generally suitable for double- and, in some areas, triple-cropping. In recent years, the region has also become home to most of Anxi's manufacturing, in numerous small-scale enterprises.

Until the 1950s, the Xi River was navigable from Hutou through Fengcheng to its confluence with the Jin River in neighboring Nanan; the Jin itself was then navigable to Quanzhou on the coast.[10] Navigation has since been interrupted by construction of dams and hydroelectric stations and by silting. Outer Anxi also has a fairly dense network of roadways, including a provincial road that connects Fengcheng (the county seat) with Quanzhou and with the Xiamen-Fuzhou highway. Fengcheng is about 58 kilometers by road from Quanzhou, and about 100 kilometers from Xiamen.[11]

Inner Anxi includes the southeastern end of the Daiyun mountain range; much of the region is at elevations of over 800 meters, with numerous peaks of 1200-1600 meters, and with steep slopes and narrow valleys. The climate is cooler and wetter than in the east, with four distinct seasons. Inner Anxi falls within the "Mountain Agricultural Zone of Central Fujian" and, within agriculture, specializes in grain and forest products, along with tea and fruits. Double-cropping of grain (typically rice—wheat) is feasible in many locales in Inner Anxi. The townships of Gande, Fengtian, Lutian, and Longjuan have Anxi's most important commercial forests, and Changkeng, Xiping, and Gande produce some of the finest Wulong teas. The northern part of inner Anxi has iron, coal, and other mineral resources. Mines near Pantian (in Gande) produce ores with iron content exceeding 55 percent, Jiandou and Weili (in Gande) produce anthracite, and Qingyang (in Shangqing) has some of the richest manganese deposits in Fujian.

Inner Anxi is generally more isolated, by the natural barriers of distance and rugged terrain, than is outer Anxi. The region's mountain streams are not generally navigable, and its road network is thin and poorly developed. Parts of the region have been oriented more toward the industrial belt of central Fujian, which use Anxi iron and coal, than toward the China coast; indeed, the city of Zhangping, one of Fujian's major rail junctions since the 1950s, is only about 25 kilometers west of the Anxi border. The Zhangping-Quanzhou rail line, a major construction project of 1980s and early 1990s, will substantially relieve the isolation of inner Anxi, and make the region much more easily accessible from the coast. As of mid 1992, several sections of this line, running from Zhangping as far as Hutou, had already been laid.[12]

Population and Migration. The people of Anxi are predominantly of the Han majority, with small numbers of the She, Zhuang, and Hui (all viewed as ethnic minorities).[13] The local language is the *Minnanyu* of Quanzhou and Xiamen—and of Taiwan.

For Anxi as a whole, population density approached 100 persons per square kilometer in the early 19th century, reached 120 in the early 1940s and again in the 1950s, and stood at well over 300 by 1990. (Of course, the density per unit of arable land is much higher, exceeding 3500 persons per square kilometer, or 2.3 per mu, by 1990.) In much of inner Anxi, densities range below 200 persons per square kilometer, as compared to densities of over 500 in parts of outer Anxi. Anxi's principal towns are located near the eastern border of the county, along the Xi and Lan Rivers. All of the towns in Anxi are of very modest size; as of 1985, Fengcheng, the largest town and the county seat, had a non-agricultural population of about 12,800 and a labor force of 8200 outside agriculture. (See Table A10, in the Appendix.)[14]

Historically, Anxi was an important hinterland for the port cities of Quanzhou and Xiamen. The county produced and exported minerals, lumber, paper, sugar—and, in particular, tea and local specialties such as persimmon cakes and bambooware.[15] Anxi's largest export, however, has been people. As of the mid 1980s, over 700,000 overseas Chinese (including Chinese in Hong Kong and Macao) traced their ancestries to Anxi, with the largest groups in Singapore, Indonesia, and Malaysia. In addition, about 2 million Taiwanese are of Anxi ancestry. As of 1986, about 180,000 residents of Anxi (22 percent of the total population) had relatives overseas or had themselves lived overseas before taking up residence in the county.[16]

Outmigration from Anxi helped stave off abject poverty among those who stayed, by relieving the pressure of a growing population upon the land. Hence, in the early 1950s, grain output per capita in Anxi was roughly on a par with that of Fujian as a whole, and marginally above the minimal requirements of the county's population.[17] Outmigration also created an external source of remittances and investment funds. During the 1930s and 1940s, for example, overseas Chinese are known to have

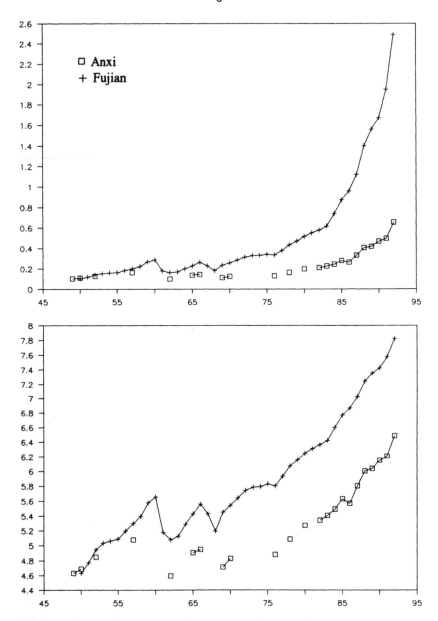

Figure 1.1. GVIAO per Capita in Anxi and Fujian, 1949-92

Note. Top: Thousands of 1980 constant yuan. Bottom: Logarithms.

Sources. For Anxi: Tables A1 and A2. For Fujian: FJTJNJ93, pp. 31, 44.

invested in transport, in a credit cooperative, and in manufacturing.[18] And, largely due to their philanthropic activities, by 1949 Anxi had 134 primary schools (with about 17,500 students) and four middle schools.[19] During the early years of the People's Republic, the Fujian provincial government actively cultivated overseas Chinese connections.[20] After the mid 1950s, however, the contributions of overseas kinfolk were severely constrained by national policies that did not permit foreign investment and, at times, victimized people tainted by foreign ties.

Despite the initiatives of the 1930's and 1940s, as of 1949 Anxi had little in the way of "modern sector" activities.[21] The county's industry was limited to a print shop, food-processing plants (notably, in the tea industry), small iron works, and handicrafts. In transport and communications, the entire county had only one motorroad (of 57 kilometers, linking Fengcheng with Tongan county), 17 bridges, and 240 kilometers of postal routes. Much of rural Anxi remained entirely dependent upon transport by wheelbarrow and shoulder-pole.

Anxi in the Provincial Economy. Figure 1.1 shows the timepaths of GVIAO (Gross Value of Industrial and Agricultural Output) per capita since 1949, for Anxi county and for Fujian province as a whole.[22] Figure 1.2 shows per capita output of grain—by far the single largest product of Anxi, by value. Both figures reveal that, as of the early and mid 1950s, Anxi was not especially poor. The figures also show that Anxi has experienced a sharp relative decline over the past four decades.[23] Since the 1950s, the GVIAO gap (in Figure 1.1) has widened almost continually, until by the 1980s Anxi's GVIAO per capita stood at less than 40 percent that of Fujian as a whole. The grain gap (in Figure 1.2), after closing entirely in the early 1960s, widened to over 100 kilograms per capita by the 1980s.

As one might expect in view of Figures 1.1 and 1.2, Anxi County has played a very modest role in the larger provincial economy. Anxi supplies iron ore from the Pantian mines, mainly to Sanming in central Fujian, and some forest products, building materials, electric power, coal, and perhaps fertilizer, mainly to other counties in Jinjiang prefecture; otherwise, Anxi has not been an important supplier of producer goods.[24] The county's traditional role as a seller of consumer goods—sugar, tea, fruits, bambooware, and handicrafts—seems to have diminished consider-ably by the 1970s. Output of sugar, in particular, probably declined between the 1950s and the mid 1970s, in line with the experiences of other sugar-producing counties in Fujian; surpluses shipped from the county would have declined more sharply than output, due to the growth of Anxi's

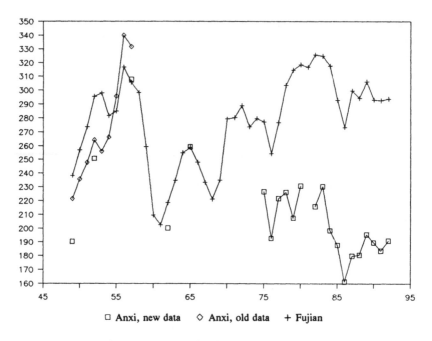

Figure 1.2. Grain Output per Capita in Anxi and Fujian, 1949-92

Note. In kilograms, unhusked. For the 1950s, two set of grain data are available. The "old" data, for 1949-57 inclusive, were released in the 1950s. The "new" data, for 1952 and 1957, were published in the 1980s. The difference between the two sets probably reflects changes in accounting conventions. In particular, potatoes were weighted 1:4 before 1963, but 1:5 thereafter (i.e., 5 kilograms of potatoes count as 1 kilogram of grain).

Sources. For Anxi: Tables A1, A5, and A7. For Fujian: FJFJ, pp. 41, 161; FJTJNJ93, pp. 44, 191.

own population.[25]   And, with the choking off of trade at Quanzhou and Xiamen between the 1950s and late 1970s due to tensions in the Taiwan Strait and to the autarkic stance of the central government, the county's products could not be readily exported.

After about 1965, Anxi's grain output per capita sank below the level of bare subsistence (i.e., around 250 kilograms per capita, unhusked), and the county became a net importer of grain—and an importer of other necessities, such as edible oil, as well. The county budget fell into deficit, requiring subsidies from the Fujian government. By the 1970s, the cost of feeding Anxi was becoming a matter of concern to provincial authorities.[26]

One of the most conspicuous and significant changes of the post-Mao era has been a restoration of Anxi's links with both the larger domestic market and with the international market. As will be shown in Chapters 3 and 4, output and export of traditional specialties have rebounded, and production of exportable manufactures—such as umbrellas, garments, and shoes—has been initiated in cooperation with foreign investors. Net inflows to the county have also increased, but appear to have been redirected, at least in part, from consumption relief to developmental assistance.

Notes

1. On Guangdong, see, e.g., Vogel, Johnson, and Nolan; see also Chan et al., and Potter and Potter. On Fujian, see Nee, Nee and Su, Nee and Young, Lyons 1992a, and Vermeer 1990. On Jiangsu, see Rozelle, Liang, and Prime; on Hebei, Putterman 1988 and Putterman 1989; on the northwest, World Bank 1990, and Vermeer 1988. See also Veeck.

2. The poverty line, in terms of rural net income per capita, is 200 yuan (of 1985). For sources and further discussion, see Lyons 1992b. For "poverty amidst plenty," e.g., FJJJ, April 1989, p. 22.

3. For many counties, the body of published material now includes new gazetteers, compiled since the mid 1980s; a complete set (one for every county in China), is due to be published by the year 2000, as part of the *Zhonghua renmin gongheguo difang zhi congshu [Collection of Local Gazetteers of the People's Republic of China]*. As of this writing, the Anxi volume is not yet available.

4. See Chapter 3.

5. Concerning "chronic poverty," see Chapter 2. For general interpretations of Maoist development, see, e.g., Reynolds, Lardy, and Lyons 1987.

6. This summary is based upon Fujian sheng cehui ju, following p. 36; Zhang and Lu, pp. 569-71; Minnan85, p. 120; and FJJJNJ87, pp. 149, 633, and map preceding p. 1.

7. The older name is retained throughout this book, to avoid confusion with the city of Quanzhou. The hierarchy of administrative regions is as follows: province; prefecture (and municipality); county (and city); town and township (or, prior to the early 1980s, commune), administrative village (or, prior to the early 1980s, brigade).

8. Weather varies sharply from year to year, however, and droughts and floods are common occurrences. For example, in 1990 a large portion of the county suffered flooding caused by typhoons; the following year, the county suffered severe drought. See, e.g, FJRB, 12 October 1990, p. 2, and FJJJNJ92, p. 441.

9. Fujian shifan daxue, pp. 143-45, 160; Cheng, p. 372.

10. Zhang and Lu, p. 577.

11. Fujian sheng jiaotong ting, p. 29.

12. See Section C in Chapter 3.

13. Minnan85, p. 119.

14. By way of comparison, the state of Rhode Island, with land area and total population comparable to those of Anxi, has a city of 160,000.

15. E.g., Fujian sheng zhengfu, pp. 209-17; Gardella, pp. 42-43.

16. FJJJNJ87, p. 633; Zhang and Lu, p. 570; FJJJNJ90, p. 466. See also FJRB, 19 January 1992, p. 5, and FJRB, 12 July 1992, p. 6.

17. See Figure 1.2, below.

18. Lin and Zhuang, pp. 176, 219, 263-64.

19. Zhang and Lu, pp. 576-80; FJJJNJ87, p. 634.

20. See, e.g., Fuzhou shi guiguo huaqiao lianyihui.

21. Zhang and Lu, p. 576; ZGGYQY, p. 782.

22. Conceptually, GVIAO is not the most desirable measure of output. It is used in this paper because it is the only measure available for years prior to the 1980s. See Chapters 2 and 4 for further comment.

23. In the 1950s, Anxi's output per capita was comparable to that of Fujian. As the data presented below suggest, Fujian was not a poor province:

GVIAO per capita (1980 yuan)	Fujian	China
1952	141	139
1957	201	207

Grain output per capita (kilograms, unhusked)		
1952	295	288
1957	306	306.

For Fujian, Figures 1.1 and 1.2; for China, SYC81, p. 17, and SY85, pp. 25, 185.

24. E.g., Li, Chen, and Yu; ZGGYQY.

25. Lardy, pp. 67-69. As of the early 1980s, Anxi planted only about 6000 mu to sugar cane. In 1983, the county produced 26,400 tons of cane, and about 2700 tons of refined sugar (about 3.5 kilograms per capita). Most of this would have been consumed locally. See Tables A6 and A7.

26. Concerning the burden of grain inflows, see, e.g., Huang, p. 263.

2

The Maoist Era

The turning point of the late 1970s (Figure 1.1) reflects fundamental changes in economic institutions and policies—changes associated with the shift from the Maoist to the post-Mao regime. This chapter focuses on the Maoist phase of Anxi's socialist development; later chapters will focus on the post-Mao phase to date. Ideally, perhaps, the dividing line between the two phases would be drawn sharply and consistently at 1979. The available data, however, do not permit this degree of precision. In this chapter and those to follow, the years 1978-83 are frequently taken as a transitional period from the first phase to the second, and data for these years are used to capture both the state of the Anxi economy at the end of the Maoist era and the state of the economy in the earliest years of reform and reopening.

A. Development Efforts

During the Maoist era, Anxi remained an overwhelmingly agrarian economy—and an economy in which collective (and household) activities loomed much larger than those of the state sector. The data in Figure 2.1 reflect the limited direct role of the state in the Anxi economy, in terms of both budgetary expenditure by the county government and investment in "basic capital construction" (BCC) by all levels of government.[1] Throughout the period from the 1950s to 1980, county budgetary expenditure—which includes mainly investment in BCC and spending for such purposes as education, health and welfare—remained below 20 yuan per capita annually, in terms of current prices. In real terms, budgetary expenditure per capita in 1980 was about three times that of 1957—an average annual growth rate of about 5 percent. The county generally ran surpluses until the late 1960s (remitting revenues to the province), and

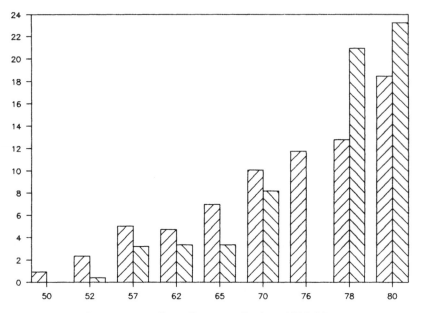

Figure 2.1. Government Spending per Capita, 1950-80

Note. In current yuan. Expenditure (shown on the left) includes on-budget spending of county government only. BCC (shown on the right) is basic capital construction by governments at county level and above.

Source. Zhang and Lu, pp. 584-85.

deficits thereafter (receiving subsidies).[2] Annual investment in BCC, by higher levels of government as well as by the county, remained below 20 yuan per capita until the late 1970s. BCC overtook county-level expenditure in the 1970s, as higher levels of government stepped up their direct investment in Anxi.

As shown in Table 2.1, government-funded investment was directed mainly toward relatively large water-control projects (some including hydroelectric power stations), government-owned tea and tree farms, "backbone" industrial enterprises, and social overhead capital projects, such as roads, bridges, the postal system, and school buildings; the burst of investment after 1978 is partly attributable to construction of the Zhangping-Quanzhou railroad (noted in Chapter 1). Government investment in infrastructure has been supplemented by collectively-organized contributions of labor and materials and, at times, by donations from overseas Chinese.

Anxi's low levels of BCC and of government expenditure in general reflect the fact that the county is overwhelmingly rural; government

Table 2.1. State Investment in Basic Capital Construction, 1950-83

Period	Amount (yuan)	Distribution
1950-52		recovery: restoring transport and communications, trade, and education
1952	134,400	
1953-57	2,597,400	63.2 percent of total used for agriculture and industry: warehouses, factories (including tea processing, electrometallurgy, liquor, agricultural machinery), flood control and irrigation; new schools and public-health facilities
1957	1,230,000	
1958-65	16,122,200	water control and erosion control; "five small industries" (including county-run cement, tile, and agricultural machinery plants, and small hydroelectric power stations)
1962	1,400,000	
1965	1,550,000	
1966-78	40,646,400	construction and expansion of factories and mines (including fertilizer, pharmaceuticals, building materials, coal, paper, food products, iron, machinery); roads; hydroelectric stations
1970	4,540,000	
1978	14,630,000	
1979-83[a]	107,000,000	construction and expansion of factories (sugar, cement, light industries); electric power; transportation and communications (including railroad and roads)
1980	13,332,100	

a. Obtained by subtracting 1952-78 sum and 1984 figure from reported 1950-84 total.

Sources. FJJJNJ87, pp. 634-35; Zhang and Lu, pp. 578, 584-85; Minnan85, p. 123.

spending in China is aimed mainly at building urban industry and securing the welfare of city people. But they are also partly attributable to provincial policies that directed investment toward other parts of Fujian. First, under the "inland development strategy" pursued during the 1960s and 1970s, Fujian's investment in industry was concentrated along the railroad running north-south in the center of the province, from Nanping to Longyan. The city of Sanming, midway along this rail corridor, became the heavy-industrial center of the province.[3] Although Anxi itself is entirely inland, it is located in a coastal prefecture and, until the mid 1980s, had no rail service. Second, the province's grain output per capita, like Anxi's, collapsed after the Great Leap Forward of the late 1950s and did not fully recover until the 1970s. As the central government constrained grain inflows to Fujian under the "grain first" policy, the Fujian government was forced to seek grain self-sufficiency; it did so partly by concentrating government aid to agriculture in the counties most likely to produce grain surpluses. These were mainly counties in the west of the province and in Longxi prefecture at the province's southern tip. The rest of the province was supposed to pursue local self-sufficiency, mainly through local efforts with very modest state assistance.[4]

Most of the investment in Anxi's agriculture and small-scale industry was undertaken by rural collectives, rather than the state. (The rural economy was collectivized in the 1950s, culminating in the formation of communes in 1958. As of 1980, Anxi had 15 communes, divided into about 240 brigades and 2500 production teams.[5]) Under a long-term policy of "comprehensive harnessing of mountains, rivers, and farmland," Anxi's rural collectives mobilized large numbers of workers for construction projects. Over 14,100 water-control projects were undertaken between 1950 and 1984, including 541 reservoirs (with a total capacity of 29.5 million cubic meters) and 158 pumping stations. The county's irrigated area increased by 52,500 mu during the First Five-Year Plan period (1953-57), and by 48,000 mu during 1958-65; by 1980, 228,000 mu (55 percent of the county's farmland) were classified as "effectively irrigated," with 91,000 mu of stable-yield area protected against both drought and flooding and with almost 28,000 kilowatts of agricultural machinery in use.[6] Labor was also mobilized for construction of small-scale factories, mines, and power plants, to be run by rural collectives. (By 1980, the county had some 300 small hydroelectric stations.[7]) Apart from hydroelectricity and the rest of the "five small industries" serving agricultural development, communes also ran enterprises in such industries as tea processing and bamboo-working—that is, simple industries using local agricultural products as inputs.[8]

Partly as a result of heavy investment in farmland capital construction, Anxi's cultivated and, especially, sown areas increased during the 1950s. Thereafter, the cultivated and sown areas probably declined gradually as farmland was taken for homes, factories, and roads, with perhaps a temporary upturn in the 1970s.[9] In fact, almost the entire increase in grain output between 1952 and 1957 can be traced to the increase in area sown to grain. The bulk of the increase in sown area, in turn, can be traced to an increase in multiple-cropping. By contrast, the increase in grain output between 1957 and 1980 is attributable entirely to increasing yield (per mu sown), since the area sown to grain decreased.[10]

Between 1957 and 1980, application of chemical fertilizer increased from very low levels to about 33,000 tons per year—41 kilograms per sown mu (or about 7.7 kilograms, in terms of nutrient content). Also over this period, improved varieties of rice were widely adopted in Fujian—and undoubtedly in Anxi, although county-level data confirming this point are not available.[11]

As elsewhere in China, labor mobilization for farmland capital construction and rural industrialization was carried to excess during the Great Leap of 1958 and during the late 1960s and early 1970s. Responding to a central initiative, the Fujian government launched a massive campaign for water control in October 1957. The county-level targets for this campaign were heavily concentrated in Jinjiang prefecture; Anxi's target for 1958, in terms of area to be irrigated, was 40,000 mu. The county reported fulfilling this target in February, and reported irrigation of 84,000 mu as of April 2.[12] These reports, to the extent that they bear any relation to reality, suggest a frenzied effort almost certainly devoid of any serious attention to potential waterlogging and salinization. Later reports also indicate that large areas of forest were destroyed in 1958, for farmland construction and to provide fuel for iron-smelting.[13] During 1966-76, overemphasis on grain farming under the prevailing "grain first" policy and the campaign to emulate Dazhai again resulted in loss of arable land, as well as loss of forested area and neglect of tea and fruit production. In Changkeng commune, for example, building 625 mu of farmfields on Hulong Mountain required 120,000 man-days of labor—and resulted in erosion on 16,249 mu, caused silting of the Buwei River, and subjected 1,800 mu to flooding.[14]

More generally, the Great Leap and the Cultural Revolution appear to have caused substantial and long-lasting damage to the Anxi economy (Figures 1.1 and 1.2). GVIAO per capita fell by 39 percent between 1957 and 1962, with most of the decrease due to the collapse of agriculture and, especially, of grain-farming.[15] Grain output fell from 118,600 tons in 1957 to just 83,700 tons in 1962. As of 1962, output of other major products of agriculture, such as tea and fruits, was also below the levels of the 1950s. The annual increment to Anxi's population, which ran at about 10,000 per year during the mid 1950s, fell to just 1365 in 1961 (Table A1); the death rate increased from about 6.5 per thousand in the mid 1950s to 13 per thousand in 1961.[16] After a recovery during 1962-65, another substantial downturn occurred during the late 1960s. GVIAO per capita was lower in 1970 than in 1965, and grain output in each of the four years 1966-69 fell below that of 1965 (Table A5). A local network for technical cooperation among communes, factories, and schools—set up in 1957—

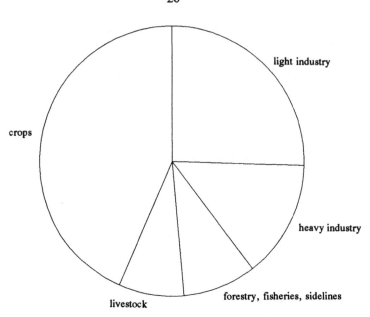

Figure 2.2. Components of GVIAO Increment, 1950-78

Note. In 1980 constant prices. All data in terms of "old" definitions (i.e., team enterprises included in agricultural sidelines). 1950 components of agriculture estimated by applying 1949 shares for branches of agriculture to 1950 GVAO; 1950 GVAO exceeds 1949 GVAO by about 9 percent. The components of GVIAO are as follows (in 1000 yuan):

	1950	1978
light industry	1270	21,750
heavy industry	20	11,350
crops	18,190	53,130
livestock	7570	13,980
forestry	640	4780
fisheries	20	40
sidelines	5310	8380.

Sources. Zhang and Lu, pp. 574, 584-85; Minnan85, pp. 207-14.

reportedly ceased to function in 1966; it did not revive until 1978.[17] The large increase in yields between the 1950s and 1980 (noted earlier) suggests, however, that agricultural extension work—and, in particular, popularization of better varieties and the farming practices associated with them—was not so seriously damaged.[18]

B. Structural Change

Economic development entails not just increases in aggregate output but also changes in the structure of output and in the constellation of productive activities yielding output. This section briefly examines the extent to which the structure of Anxi's economy changed, prior to the 1980s.

Sectoral Composition of Output. Figure 2.2 decomposes the increment in GVIAO between 1950 and 1978 into five components. Heavy industry accounted for only 14.1 percent of the total increment; in fact, heavy industry became a significant component of Anxi's GVIAO only in the 1970s.[19] By contrast, the crop-farming branch of agriculture accounted for 43.5 percent of the increment, and the crop and livestock branches together for over 50 percent. Most of the rest originated in light industry and in rural sidelines (including team-run collective enterprises). As of 1978, Anxi's agriculture lagged behind the rest of the province—GVAO per capita of 114 yuan (in 1980 constant prices) in Anxi, as compared to 174 yuan in Fujian as whole.[20] Anxi's industry was far less developed—GVIO per capita of 47 yuan, as compared to 266 in Fujian as a whole. Indeed, the level of industrial development attained by Anxi in 1978 is comparable to that attained by some rural areas of Fujian during the 1950s.[21]

Labor Force and Employment. Detailed sectoral breakdowns of Anxi's labor force are not available for years prior to the 1980s. The available data (collected in Table A1) do indicate that, although the number of "workers and staff" employed by government and by urban collectives increased by a factor of about six between the mid 1950s and late 1970s, workers and staff still accounted for only about 11 percent of the labor force as of 1978. A substantial portion of Anxi's workers and staff reside in the towns of Fengcheng, Guanqiao, and Hutou (Table A10).

Agriculture. Table 2.2 provides a more detailed look at the predominant crop and livestock branches of agriculture at the end of the Maoist era.[22] The ratio of grain crops (mainly rice, but also wheat and sweet potatoes) to "economic," or cash, crops (mainly peanuts, sugar cane, and tobacco) is over 20:1 in terms of sown area, with the share of grain in sown area ranging up to 91 percent. And the area devoted to tea and fruit orchards is notably small—about 100,000 mu were planted to tea as of the early 1980s, and 20,000-30,000 mu to fruits (oranges, longan and litchi, plums, and persimmon).

Table 2.2. Structure of Crop and Livestock Production, 1980-84

	1980	1982	1983	1984
Cultivated Area (1000 mu)	411.3		410	407.7
Sown Area (1000 mu)	817.3	807	797.5	780.9
grain	744.2	722	719.2	688.4
economic crops		36	28.5	39.1
other crops		49	49.8	
Tea Area (1000 mu)	97			104
Fruit Area (1000 mu)				27
Yearend Stocks (1000)				
cattle				51.8
pigs	193.3		233.9	234.7
poultry				1240

Note: For greater detail on crops, see the Appendix.

Sources. For areas: Table A6. For livestock: Minnan85, pp. 122, 218-19; Zhang and Lu, p. 575.

Per mu of sown area, Anxi's grain output was about 9 percent below that of Fujian as a whole, as of 1980. Per mu of cultivated area, however, Anxi's output was only 5 percent below Fujian's, reflecting somewhat greater double-cropping of grain in Anxi. Anxi's yields for cash crops (peanuts and sugar) and tree crops (fruits) are also slightly below those for Fujian, perhaps reflecting general neglect, relegation of these crops to marginal lands, and scattered, small-scale operations. Even in tea, Anxi's traditional specialty crop, yields fell below the provincial average; some reports suggest that tea production was widely scattered in sideline operations rather than in the large specialized farms more likely to acquire and deploy modern inputs and techniques.[23]

As shown in Table 2.2, by the early 1980s Anxi had substantial pig and poultry industries. These industries are based mainly on farmyard feeding (with a pig or two, and a few chickens or ducks, per household), and are complementary to grain-farming, in that the livestock eat milling byproducts and are themselves a source of fertilizer. Fisheries, not shown in the table, were not developed to any appreciable extent until the 1980s.

Table 2.3. Structure of Industrial Output, 1980 and 1984

	1980		1984	
	value[b]	share[c]	value[b]	share[c]
GVIO[a]	43,500	100	54,830	100
light industry	28,160	65	36,760	67
processing products of				
agriculture			32,370	59
other			4,390	8
heavy industry	15,340	35	18,070	33
mining			990	1.8
raw materials			10,180	18.6
manufacturing			6,900	12.6
GVIO[a]	43,500	100	54,830	100
food products	18,270	42	28,350	51.7
chemicals	4,790	11	5,810	10.6
building materials			4,610	8.4
electrical power	3,480	8	3,670	6.7
machine-building	6,530	15	3,320	5.9
educational/cultural materials			2,470	4.5
paper			1,700	3.1
forest products			1,540	2.8
garments			1,100	2
coal			660	1.2
metallurgy			550	1
leather			220	0.4
other			930	1.7

Note: See also Table 4.5.

a. Gross Value of Industrial and Agricultural Output.

b. In thousands of 1980 constant yuan; "old" coverage: excludes sidelines at team and household levels.

c. In percent.

Sources. Fujian sheng cehui ju, following p. 36; Fujian shehui kexue yuan, pp. 246-48.

Overall, the data in Table 2.2 are consistent with local claims of overwhelming emphasis on grain production during much of the Maoist era, with other agricultural activities suppressed or, at best, viewed as sidelines rather than as legitimate objects of specialization.

Table 2.4. Major Enterprises in Anxi, 1978-84

1. Industrial Enterprises with Output Value Exceeding 1 Million Yuan in 1984

> Anxi Tea Factory (Guanqiao)
> Anxi County Sugar Mill (Fengcheng)
> Fuqian Tea Factory (operated by Fuqian tea farm in Fengtian)
> Chengxiang Grain and Oil Processing Plant
> Anxi County Cement Plant (Jiandou)
> Hutou Cement Plant (operated by Jinjiang Prefecture)
> Shangqing Bamboo Products Plant (operated by Shangqing Commune)
> Anxi Pharmaceuticals Plant (Fengcheng)
> Anxi Chemical Fertilizer Plant (Jiandou)
> Anxi Distillery (Fengcheng)
> Anxi Paper Mill (Gande)

2. Other "Backbone" Enterprises

> Panluo Iron District (operates Anxi's Pantian and Zhangping's Luoyang
>   mines)
> Anxi Electrometallurgical Plant
> Xianrong Power Plant (operated by Jinjiang Prefecture)
> Jiandou Power Plant
> Cunnei Power Station (Longmen)
> Jianan Power Station
> Fujian #1 Highway Construction Company (Fengcheng)
> Tiefeng Stone Company (Guanqiao)
> Anxi Pine Rosin Factory (Xiping)
> Lutian Tea Factory (operated by the Lutian tea farm)
> Xiping Tea Processing Plant (operated by Xiping township)
> Huqiu Tea Processing Company (operated by Huqiu township)
> Anxi Food Products Factory (Fengcheng)
> Anxi Chemical-Industry Equipment Factory
> agricultural machinery factory

Sources. For list #1: Zhang and Lu, pp. 576, 578. For list #2: Chen Jilin, p. 71; Fujian sheng cehui ju, following p. 36; Minnan85, pp. 123, 157; FJJJNJ85, pp. 710-11; FJJJNJ86, p. 739; FJJJNJ87, pp. 140, 832. See also Table A9.

Industry. Table 2.3 shows the structure of Anxi's industrial output in 1980 and 1984.[24] As of 1980, the food-products branch was far and away the most important—and tea processing was the most important food-products industry. (Since most grain is milled in villages, grain-processing is largely excluded from GVIO.) Machine-building was second in importance, producing mainly agricultural machinery, such as irrigation pumps and tea-processing equipment. The chemical branch produced mainly pharmaceuticals, nitrogenous and phosphate fertilizers, and calcium carbide. In the more detailed breakdown for 1984 (in Table 2.3), the general contours of the 1980 structure are still evident. The building materials industry—8.4 percent of GVIO in 1984—produces mainly cement, tiles, and fireproofing materials; the mining industry (apparently included in "other" in the table) produces mainly iron ore.[25] In both 1980 and 1984, the industrial structure of Anxi clearly reflects the importance of industries that process outputs of local agriculture and that produce inputs to agriculture and to farmland capital construction.

As of 1978, Anxi had only 64 industrial enterprises operated by various levels of government or by communes. By 1984, this number had increased to 168, with 71 million yuan in fixed assets and 15,000 employees.[26] As shown in Table 2.4, only eleven of these enterprises produced over 1 million yuan in output value; collectively, these accounted for 63 percent of the county's GVIO. Most of the eleven were developed with state investment over the course of the Maoist era. For example, the Anxi Tea Factory—probably the county's largest industrial enterprise during 1978-84—was established in 1952. After several expansion and modernization projects, the plant occupied 47,000 square meters and employed 1459 people by the mid 1980s. The Fujian #1 Highway Construction Company, also one of the largest enterprises in Anxi, is a construction, rather than industrial, enterprise; hence, the bulk of its output is not included in GVIO and GVIAO. Established in 1963, the company has built a number of important roads and bridges in Anxi and in other counties; as of the mid 1980s, it employed over 2000 people.[27]

Most of the larger enterprises shown in Table 2.4 are located in the eastern towns of Fengcheng, Hutou, and Guanqiao, which accounted for about half of Anxi's GVIO in the mid 1980s (Table A10). Some of the important tea-processing plants, and the principal iron-mining district, are located farther to the west. Apart from these relatively large enterprises, by 1984 Anxi also had about 4,000 scattered village enterprises (the output of which is included in the sideline branch of agriculture, rather than in the non-agricultural sectors). These produced, on average, gross income of less than 1500 yuan each.[28]

Table 2.5. Commercialization and Related Infrastructure, 1978-84

	1978	1980	1983	1984
Commercial Outlets[a]				
total				635
per 1000 persons				0.8
				(0.9)
Roads				
total (kilometers)	714			1048
per km^2	0.24			0.35
	(0.24)			(0.29)
Vehicles[b]				
total				2187
per 1000 persons				2.8
				(n.a.)
Telephones				
total				1100[c]
per 1000 persons				1.4
				(4.7)
Retail Sales				
total (million current yuan)	50.09	63.51	90.71	100.14
per capita (current yuan)	72	88	119	142
	(152)	(215)	(274)	(317)
as share of GVIAO (percent)[d]	47	46	50	54
	(37)	(43)	(42)	(40)
Exports[e]				
total (million current yuan)	7.39	9.97	12.31	13.28
per capita (current year)	11	14	16	17
	(19)			(37)
as share of GVIAO (percent)[d]	7.0	7.2	6.8	6.5
	(4.7)			(4.7)
Net Domestic Purchases[f]				
total (million current yuan)				46.85
as share of GVIAO (percent)[d]				23
				(27)
State Procurement of Grain				
tons (gross)			3516	5299
as share of output (percent)			2.0	3.4
			(18)	(18)

Table 2.5, continued

	1978	1980	1983	1984
Freight Transportation[g]				
total (1000 tons originated)	190.5	340.0		230.0[h]
per capita (kilograms)	270	467		
	(1980)	(2060)		
Telecommunications Business				
total (1000 current yuan)				660
per capita (current yuan)				0.8
				(2.7)

Note: Figures in parentheses are the corresponding ratios for Fujian province.

a. Includes only outlets operated by government or by supply and marketing cooperatives.

b. Includes trucks, buses, cars, motorcycles, tractors, and hand-tractors (many of which are converted for use as vehicles).

c. 1985.

d. GVIAO: Gross Value of Industrial and Agricultural Output.

e. Purchase of goods for export by foreign trade departments; for further detail, see Table 3.1.

f. I.e., purchases of commodities by agents in the commercial sector from agents (factories, etc.) outside the sector; includes only purchases by the state commercial system and by supply and marketing cooperatives.

g. By transport departments only.

h. Decline reflects shift from transport departments to private and cooperative transport companies.

Sources. For Anxi GVIAO and population: Tables A1 and A2; GVIAO converted to current-price basis using provincial deflator, in FJFJ, pp. 22-23. For provincial population and GVIAO, Figure 1.1 and FJFJ, p. 22. For commercial outlets: Minnan85, p. 124; FJTJNJ86, p. 176. For roads and vehicles: Zhang and Lu, p. 577; FJFJ, p. 79. For telephones: Minnan86, p. 139; FJSHTJ, p. 91. For Anxi retail sales: Zhang and Lu, pp. 584-85; Minnan85, p. 227. For Fujian retail sales: FJFJ, p. 90. For exports: Minnan85, p. 228; FJJJNJ85, p. 202. For net domestic purchases: Zhang and Lu, p. 578; FJFJ, p. 93. For Anxi grain procurement: unpublished data collected by Bruce Stone, International Food Policy Research Institute. For Fujian grain procurement: Lyons 1993, p. 705. For Anxi and Fujian grain output: Figure 1.2. For transport: Zhang and Lu, pp. 584-85; FJFJ, p. 81. For telecommunications: Minnan85, p. 123; FJFJ, p. 83.

Table 2.6. Education, Health, and Related Infrastructure, 1964-84

	1964	1978	1982	1984
Schools				
elementary				382
middle[a]				26
Teachers[b]				5738
Students Attending (1000)	56.0[c]	128.8		138.0
Enrollment Rate (percent)[d]				95.8
Health-care Facilities				42
Hospital Beds				
total		482		601
per 1000 persons		0.68		0.77
Health-care Workers[e]				
total		537		801
per 1000 persons		0.76		1.13
Illiteracy Rate (percent)[f]	65.4		49.7	
Lower Middle School Graduates[g]				
total (1000)	21.1		94.5	
per 1000 persons	46		124	
Technicians[h]				3691
Infant Mortality (per 1000)			29	
Life Expectancy at Birth (years)				
male			63.7[i]	
female			67.4[i]	

a. Includes vocational middle schools.

b. Teachers and staff in elementary and middle schools (but not vocational middle schools).

c. 1965.

d. Share of school-age children entering school, whether or not they continue in school.

e. Full-time health-care specialists, including doctors; excludes rural (generally part-time) health-care workers.

f. Number illiterate or semi-literate (generally defined as recognizing fewer than 1,500 characters), as share of the population over 12 years of age.

g. Those with *at least* lower middle school (including those with more).

Table 2.6, continued

h. Those with technical training at middle school level and/or actually employed as technicians.

i. 1981.

Sources. For schools, teachers, and students: Zhang and Lu, pp. 580, 584-85; Minnan85, p. 124. For health-care facilities, beds, and workers: Minnan85, pp. 125, 242-43. For illiteracy, lower-middle graduates, infant mortality, and life expectancy: FJRKTJ, pp. 316, 318, 320, 326-27, 331; Population Census Office, p. 175. For number of technicians: Zhang and Lu, p. 582.

C. Social Overhead Capital

Tables 2.5 and 2.6 look beyond the agricultural and industrial sectors, to examine (1) the infrastructures supporting commerce and delivery of social services, and (2) the extent of commercialization and the levels of education and health attained by the late 1970s and early 1980s. Most of the investment reflected in these tables occurred after 1952; as shown above, Anxi inherited a very small stock of social overhead capital from the pre-war era.

As shown in Table 2.5, by the end of the Maoist era, Anxi had about 700 kilometers of motorroads and almost 2200 vehicles of various sorts (including 344 trucks). The density of Anxi's road network was comparable to that of Fujian as a whole. Anxi, however, enjoyed neither rail service nor river navigation of any significance; hence, the overall availability of transport, and of low-cost long-distance transport in particular, was lower than in Fujian as a whole. Many villages in the county remained inaccessible by motor vehicle. Telephone service remained extremely limited countywide. Indeed, as late as 1985, ten of the thirty villages in Penglai (one of Anxi's five towns) still had no telephone service.[29]

Government-operated establishments (along with supply and marketing cooperatives, subject to close government control) still dominated Anxi's commerce in the early 1980s. In addition, a substantial portion of Anxi's trade was conducted at traditional periodic markets, with at least one such market in each town and township. Most operate every third or fifth day.[30]

Some of the performance measures in Table 2.5 are surprising, given the state of Anxi's infrastructure and Anxi's low level of development. On a per capita basis, retail sales are low—as one would expect, given the level of development in the county. But retail sales in Anxi actually ran ahead of those for Fujian as a whole in 1980, when standardized by GVIAO rather than population. This probably reflects the importance of subsidies to the county and remittances to many of its households, which serve to divorce the level of consumption from earned incomes and, therefore, from local production. The relatively high share of exports in GVIAO reflects Anxi's importance in the tea industry, and especially in the production of Tieguanyin and other high-quality Wulong teas much in demand on the international market; Wulong tea was Fujian's fifth largest export by value, as of 1978.[31] The low "grain commodity rate" (about 3 percent for 1983/84) reflects the fact that Anxi is seriously grain-deficit and that little locally-produced grain is available for redistribution within the county.[32]

Table 2.6 suggests that medical and educational services improved markedly over the course of the Maoist era, with the addition of over 250 schools and 36 health-care facilities. As of 1978-84, almost all of the school-age children of Anxi had access to elementary education; some sources, however, report low retention rates, beyond the first year or two of schooling.[33] And the quality of schooling was apparently quite low in many areas, with poorly trained teachers and shortages of books, equipment, and classrooms.[34] As of 1978-84, a substantial portion of Anxi's people had ready access to health care, through a network of township- and village-level facilities centered upon the county hospital in Fengcheng. In addition to the health-care professionals shown in the table, Anxi also had 847 "qualified rural health-care workers."[35]

The cumulative effect of investment in social services is reflected in the attainment indicators at the bottom of Table 2.6. Despite the substantial improvement in the educational system, about 50 percent of Anxi's population aged 12 and over were still functionally illiterate as of 1982, as compared to 37 percent for the province as a whole. Lower-middle-school graduates and technicians amounted to only about 12 percent and 0.5 percent of Anxi's total population, respectively. In contrast to the sorry state of educational attainment, the health of Anxi's population appears to be much better than the general level of development in Anxi would lead one to expect. Although infant mortality in Anxi is higher, and life expectancy shorter, than in Fujian as a whole, the county compares favorably with such "upper-middle income" countries as South Korea, Malaysia, and Brazil, and with the "middle income" countries as a group.[36] This performance in Anxi is probably attributable to nearly universal provision of rudimentary health services in the countryside, to the eradication of smallpox and other diseases once prevalent in the county, and to relatively egalitarian distribution of food supplies under the collective regime.[37]

D. Welfare

The ultimate objective of Anxi's development effort during the Maoist era was improvement in the welfare of Anxi residents. Ideally, welfare would be examined using household-level data (on, e.g., changes in income, savings, consumption, and health). Lacking such data, this section tries to draw some conclusions from (1) countywide output per capita, (2) countywide income, consumption, and savings per capita, and (3) bits of evidence concerning the incidence of poverty.

After twenty-odd years of effort, Anxi's GVIAO per capita was not significantly higher in 1976-78 than in the 1950s, as shown in Figure 1.1. The fragmentary data collected in the figure suggest a pattern of violent fluctuations over the course of the Maoist era, with a mean of roughly 140 yuan per capita (in 1980 constant prices), with one peak of perhaps 180 (probably in 1958) and with one trough below 100 (probably in 1962).[38]

GVIAO is a relatively poor indicator of level of development, because it covers only the industrial and agricultural sectors and because it admits double-counting (to an extent that varies between sectors and among branches). GVIAO is used here simply because it is the only indicator available for years prior to the 1980s. Table 2.7 collects some alternative—and superior—indicators for 1983-85, and compares Anxi to the rest of Fujian. Social Gross Value (SGV) covers all five "material-producing" sectors; it is equal to GVIAO *plus* the gross values originating in construction, transport, and commerce. Rural Social Value (RSV) and Net Material Product (NMP) are derived from SGV, the former by excluding output that originates outside villages, the second by netting out double-counting. Gross Domestic Product (GDP) is broader in coverage than NMP, mainly by inclusion of more services, and, like NMP, is a value-added measure (i.e., nets out double-counting). By all five *output* indicators in Table 2.7, Anxi was very poor relative to Fujian as a whole, with output per capita of about two-fifths that of the province.[39] Indeed, a huge gap had opened between the richest and poorest areas of Fujian by the 1980s: as of 1984-85, Anxi's NMP per capita was only about 28 percent that of rich counties such as Taining and Jiangle. As shown in the last column (for those indicators where complete sets of county data are available), Anxi ranked last among Fujian's 67 counties and cities in output per capita.

In the late 1970s, Anxi was one of eleven "chronically" poverty-stricken counties in Fujian—counties with distributed collective rural *income* of less than 50 yuan per capita in all three years, 1977-79.[40] As of 1983-1985, Anxi was still among the poorest counties in the province; in fact, Anxi ranked dead last in 1983 and 1984 and third from the bottom in 1985,

Table 2.7. Output, Income, and Savings Per Capita, 1983-85

	Yuan	Percent[a]	Rank[b]
GVIAO[c]			
1983	225	36.4	67
1984	243	33.0	
1985	279	32.0	67
Social Gross Value[d]			
1985	459	35.8	
Rural Social Value[d]			
1985	327[e]	46.6	
Net Material Product[d]			
1983	173	42.9	
1984	200	41.3	67
1985	240	39.3	67
Gross Domestic Product[d]			
1985	267	37.7	
Net Rural Income[d]			
1983	180[e]	59.6	67
1984	220[e]	63.8	67
1985	269[e]	67.9	65
Savings Deposits			
1983	55.7	56.9	
1984	77.6	58.5	

a. Anxi, relative to Fujian.

b. Out of 67; Putian city included in Putian county in 1985.

c. Gross Value of Industrial and Agricultural Output, in 1980 constant prices.

d. Current prices.

e. Agricultural population only.

Sources. For Anxi GVIAO and population, Tables A1 and A2. For Anxi social gross value and GDP: Fujian shehui kexue yuan, pp. 22, 129. For Anxi NMP: Minnan85, p. 182; FJJJNJ86, p. 622. For Anxi rural income: Minnan85, p. 125; FJJJNJ86, p. 628. For Anxi savings deposits: Minnan85, p. 237. For Fujian: Figure 1.1; FJTJNJ91, p. 430; FJTJNJ92, pp. 18, 23, 29, 40-41, 363.

in terms of rural net income per capita—income from all sources, not just collective (Table 2.7). The last item in the table is a crude indicator of wealth, rather than of income. The relative gap between Anxi and Fujian

Table 2.8. Rural Poverty, 1985

	Total Number	<100 yuan[a] number	<100 yuan[a] share (%)	<150 yuan[a] number	<150 yuan[a] share (%)	<200 yuan[a] number	<200 yuan[a] share (%)
Townships[b]	20					10[c]	50[c]
Villages	429	30[c]	7[c]	111[c]	26[c]		
Households[d]	139,000					58,482	42
Persons[d]	748,100					313,768	42

a. Columns show number, and share of corresponding total, falling below the indicated net income per capita (in current yuan).

b. Includes three towns (*zhen*), in addition to seventeen townships (*xiang*).

c. 1984.

d. Agricultural only.

Sources. FJJJ, November 1988, p. 29; FJJJNJ88, p. 517.

as a whole is smaller for income and wealth than for output, reflecting subsidies and remittances.

In 1985, the counties of Fujian conducted household surveys to ascertain the extent of absolute poverty. The number of poverty-stricken rural households in Anxi far exceeded that in any other county, by the prevailing standard of 200 yuan per capita, and the share of Anxi's rural households living in poverty exceeded that in all but one other county (Fuan, in northeastern Fujian). As shown in Table 2.8, poverty was spread widely throughout Anxi: half of the county's townships and a substantial portion of its villages were poverty-stricken. Poverty in some villages was extreme; for example, in Shuigang (in Changkeng township), the great majority of households had net incomes below 100 yuan per capita in 1984, with the lowest incomes ranging down to 50-odd yuan per capita.[41]

Apart from the indicators of output, income, and wealth in Tables 2.7 and 2.8, low levels of educational and health attainment (relative to the averages for the province) might also be viewed as indicative of poverty in Anxi. As noted earlier, however, the levels attained in Fujian as a whole, and in Anxi, are far better than those one would expect in a poor rural area, based on the experiences of other countries with similarly low levels of output and income.

E. Summary and Concluding Comments

The turn-around in Anxi's fortunes in the 1980s, shown in Figure 1.1, clearly suggests that Anxi was not somehow fated to poverty by forces beyond the control of man. Rather, Anxi's sorry plight resulted primarily from policies that seriously distorted its development path. In essence, the county was trapped between the increasing pressure of population upon its land and a policy regime that constrained *both* outmigration and creation of alternative local income streams.

Anxi's population more than doubled between 1950 and 1978; its cultivated area decreased by about 6 percent over the same period. Hence, roughly 2.3 times as many people looked to each mu of farmland for their livelihoods in 1978 as compared to 1952—causing, inevitably, substantial underemployment. No credible estimate of the extent of the surplus-labor problem, circa 1978, is available. Reports of the late 1980s and early 1990s, however, point to a labor surplus of almost 60,000—16 percent of the rural labor force.[42] The surplus of 1978 was certainly much larger, since off-farm job creation in the 1980s outpaced growth of the labor force. Substantial underemployment brought with it low incomes—and, hence, low savings.

With increasing population pressure and, especially, decreasing output of grain per capita, the county's decision-makers became preoccupied with securing food supplies. But even with massive efforts at farmland capital construction and modernization (with powered irrigation, chemical fertilizers, and improved varieties), grain output still failed to keep pace with population. The increasingly desperate quest for food—and for fuel and other necessities of life—led communities to strip hillsides of vegetation, to destroy forests, and to fill ponds and wetlands. Anxi's forest cover and timber reserves fell rapidly (Table 1.1). The eroded area increased, to 809,400 mu as of 1985. The Xi and other streams became silt-laden, and some reservoirs and hydro stations had to be taken out of service due to silting problems.[43]

Given a relative scarcity of farmland and an abundance of other resources, why didn't Anxi shift toward other income-generating activities? To some extent, it did: in particular, the county invested in tea- and fruit-processing and made a start toward developing other consumer-goods industries (rattan- and bamboo-working, furniture-making) dependent for their inputs upon abundant forest resources and uplands, rather than farmfields. These industries are labor-intensive, do not require elaborate structures and equipment, and use simple technologies that can be readily diffused. But their development is inherently limited by the extent of the market—which the larger context of Maoist development severely constrained. China's autarkic stance constrained the export market, and its policies of local self-sufficiency and asceticism constrained the domestic market for non-essentials such as Anxi's persimmon cakes and rattan furniture. Furthermore, diverting labor from agriculture—even labor of low marginal productivity—requires that Anxi have continuing and secure access to an external supply of food. The Maoist policy of "grain first" explicitly limited such access.

A second, relatively small, portion of Anxi's industrial sector produces raw materials such as iron ore for export outside the county, mainly to the city of Sanming. This sector clearly increases local incomes; unfortunately, raw materials have been grossly underpriced by the Chinese planning regime, substantially reducing the extent to which export of such materials benefitted Anxi. And—perhaps in part due to the disincentives created by underpricing—the raw-material branches were not aggressively developed.

The rest of Anxi's industrial sector does not produce goods for direct consumption by the local population or for export from the county. Rather, it produces goods used as inputs to Anxi's agricultural sector. This portion of Anxi's industry can increase local welfare only to the extent that it (1) contributes to net increases in agricultural output, and/or (2) brings into Anxi resources that the county would not otherwise have received (in the form, for example, of industrial wages paid by higher levels of government). The contribution to agricultural output is reflected in the increasing yields noted earlier. The injection of resources from outside the county cannot be measured with the data at hand; however, it was probably quite modest, because the bulk of Anxi's industry is owned and operated by the county and by local collectives, not by the province and prefecture.

The general contours of Anxi's experience prior to the late 1970s reflect key elements of the "Maoist strategy"—incessant battling against nature; striving after local self-reliance and self-sufficiency; "dualistic" development of industry, involving both relatively modern government-operated factories in towns and collectively-financed rural workshops closely linked to agriculture; stunted development of commerce and the supporting infrastructure; and local egalitarianism.[44] Anxi appears to be a case in which the Maoist strategy, faithfully implemented, failed to induce sustained growth. Indeed, important strands of the strategy (such as self-sufficiency) contributed directly to stagnation and poverty, by forcing Anxi onto an unsustainable development path.

While on the one hand the Maoist strategy contributed to stagnation and poverty, on the other hand the Maoist safety net ameliorated the suffering that Anxi's poverty would otherwise have entailed. Anxi became increasingly dependent upon higher levels of government to support current budgetary expenditures—with, for example, a county budgetary deficit (i.e., subsidies from the province) running to almost 36 percent of expenditure in 1980 and 39 percent in 1983.[45] In essence, much of the assistance Anxi received constituted a consumption subsidy, providing food for the destitute and basic "social" consumption, such as health services.

The plight of Anxi prior to the 1980s cannot be laid entirely, or even primarily, to decisions made *within* the county. Rather, the fate of the county was sealed by larger decisions that cut off trade and severely constrained factor mobility. Given these larger decisions, perhaps Anxi could have better conserved its forest resources, built better roads, imparted better skills to its farmers. But without trade, no options open to the county could have rescued it from the overburdening of its farmland and the low incomes that entails. And without more capital and skills from the outside, no options open to the county could have overcome the continuing lack of local savings and expertise.

Notes

1. "Basic capital construction" (BCC) is one of two major categories of investment in fixed assets. BCC includes construction of completely new facilities, expansion of existing facilities, and purchase of equipment associated with such projects. The other major category is technical updating and transformation, which covers modernization of existing facilities. BCC accounted for the bulk of state investment in fixed assets in Fujian—over 80 percent in 1979, and probably a higher share in earlier years; FJTJNJ92, pp. 190, 193, 208.

2. For county revenues and expenditures, see Zhang and Lu, pp. 584-85; and FJJJNJ87, p. 635. Real growth is estimated by applying the provincial retail price index, as given in FJTJNJ93, p. 133; the growth rate is estimated from initial and terminal years only (i.e., 1957 and 1980).

3. On the inland strategy in Fujian, see Weng.

4. Lyons 1992a.

5. The number of communes pertains to 1980; Fujian sheng cehui ju, following p. 36. The numbers of brigades and teams are estimated by applying the numbers of brigades and teams per commune in Fujian to the number of communes in Anxi. In addition to 15 communes, in 1980 Anxi had two towns (*zhen*) and several state farms. In the early 1980s, Anxi's 15 communes were dismantled, and the traditional units of local government were reestablished. As of 1985, Anxi had seventeen townships (*xiang*) and five towns (*zhen*), as shown in the map at the front of this volume.

6. Zhang and Lu, p. 574; FJJJNJ87, p. 634; Fujian sheng cehui ju, following p. 36; ZGFX80-87, p. 205. See Tables 3.3 and 3.4, below.

7. Fujian sheng cehui ju, following p. 36.

8. The "five small industries" are energy, farm chemicals, building materials, iron, and farm tools and machines.

9. For Anxi data, see Table A5. For Fujian as a whole, cultivated area turned up slightly in 1972—the only increase between 1967 and 1985; FJJJNJ86, p. 81.

10. The data (using the "new" grain output series, for comparability between the 1950s and 1980), are as follows:

	output (tons)	sown area (mu)	yield (kg/mu)	multiple cropping index
1952	81,546	592,104	137.7	1.44
1957	118,608	870,912	136.2	1.95
1980	166,892	744,159	224.3	1.99.

Using the "old" output series for the 1950s yields virtually the same result, for 1952-57. See Tables A5, A6, and A7.

11. For fertilizer use in Anxi as of 1980, ZGFX80-87, p. 205 (in terms of nutrient content); for comparison with Fujian in the 1950s, converted to actual weight, using conversion factor of 5.3 for Anxi in 1983, as provided by Bruce Stone, International Food Policy Research Institute. In Fujian as a whole, fertilizer use totalled: 37,000 tons, or 1.2 kilograms per sown mu, in 1952; 107,000 tons, or 3.0 kilograms, in 1957; and 1,806,000 tons, or 47 kilograms, in 1980 (all in terms of actual weight); FJNYDQ, p. 403; FJTJNJ89, pp. 95, 98, 117.

12. Falkenheim, pp. 306, 314. Falkenheim's source is FJRB.

13. FJJJNJ87, p. 634.

14. Dazhai, a brigade in Shaanxi, was held up as a national model of farmland construction through massive labor mobilization. Concerning Changkeng, FJJJ, November 1988, p. 30. Efforts were made to repair damage to forest area through separate mobilization campaigns aimed at afforestation; e.g., Zhang and Lu, p. 575.

15. GVAO (in 1980 constant prices): 1957, 53.84 million yuan; 1962, 32.83 million yuan; see Table A2.

16. FJRKTJ, p. 142.

17. FJJJNJ87, p. 534; Zhang and Lu, p. 582.

18. Total grain output was at least 22 percent higher in 1975 than in 1969; see Table A5.

19. Zhang and Lu, pp. 584-85.

20. GVAO (Gross Value of Agricultural Output) and GVIO (Gross Value of Industrial Output) are the two components of GVIAO. These components are susceptible to the deficiencies of GVIAO, noted in Section 2.D, below.

21. For example, GVIO per capita in Tongan county was over 40 yuan (in 1980 constant prices) in 1957; Zhang and Lu, p. 163.

22. As noted earlier, data limitations require our looking into the early 1980s, rather than solely at the end of the Maoist era, c1979. The data in Table 2.2, therefore, capture some post-Mao changes already in progress by 1984.

23. E.g., Zhang and Lu, p. 574.

24. Again, data limitations require looking beyond the end of the Maoist era; the data in Table 2.3 capture changes of the early post-Mao years. The major post-Mao changes affecting Anxi's industry, however, gathered force only after about 1984.

25. Zhang and Lu, p. 576; Fujian sheng cehui ju, following p. 36; Chen Jiayuan, p. 257.

26. Zhang and Lu, p. 576. Commune enterprises generally became township enterprises, with the abandonment of the commune system in the mid 1980s.

27. Concerning Anxi Tea, FJJJNJ87, pp. 831; ZGQYGK, pp. 354-55. Concerning Fujian #1 Highway Construction Company, FJJJNJ87, p. 832; during 1969-73, this company was taken over by the PLA's Fujian Construction Corps.

28. Minnan85, p. 122.

29. Li, Chen, and Yu, pp. 392, 394.

30. FJJJ, November 1988, p. 31.

31. FJFJ, p. 106.

32. The "commodity rate," a widely cited measure of commercialization in grain-producing areas, is the share of total grain output that is purchased from farmers. This share has been controlled via grain procurement targets handed down by government.

33. E.g., FJJJ, November 1988, p. 30.

34. As of 1984, about 21 percent of the primary-school teachers in Anxi had not completed upper-middle school; Zhang and Lu, p. 581. In some areas, primary-school teachers had completed only primary school themselves; FJJJ, November 1988, p. 30.

35. Minnan85, p. 125.

36. World Bank 1984, pp. 218-19, 262-63. Data (for 1982) are as follows:

	Brazil	Korea	Malaysia	middle-income countries
infant mortality	63	32	29	76
life expectancy, male	62	64	65	58
life expectancy, female	66	71	69	62.

For Fujian, FJSHTJ, pp. 22, 25. (Fujian, viewed as a country in itself, would rank in the low-income group.)

37. Zhang and Lu, p. 581.

38. GVIAO per capita in 1952 and 1957: 127 and 161 yuan; GVIAO per capita in 1976 and 1978: 131 and 162 yuan. GVIAO per capita was probably higher in 1958 than in 1957; GVIAO in 1962 was 99 yuan. All data are given in 1980 constant prices. See Figure 1.1.

39. Anxi does better by the value-added measures, as compared to GVIAO. This is because (1) the share of industry is relatively small in Anxi, and (2) gross value indicators admit more double-counting in industry than in agriculture.

40. Nongye bu renmin gongshe guanli ju, pp. 119-20.

41. FJJJ, November 1988, p. 29; the Shuigang data pertain to 1984.

42. E.g., FJRB, 5 June 1991, p. 3. Of course, the labor surplus, c1978, was disguised by the collective regime, under which everyone was nominally employed.

43. FJJJ, November 1988, pp. 29-30; Fujian sheng cehui ju, following p. 36. See also FJRB, 10 November 1987, p. 2.

44. E.g., Riskin.

45. See Table 3.2, below.

3
The Post-Mao Era:
Reform and Reopening

During the closing years of the Maoist era, Anxi—still heavily dependent upon fieldcrop production—suffered underemployment, environmental degradation, and widespread poverty. Then, in the late 1970s and early 1980s, China's "reform and reopening" suddenly created an array of new opportunities for the county. Did the Anxi government formulate and implement a coherent bundle of measures—both direct government actions (e.g., spending for infrastructure) and inducements to other actors (e.g, through its tax codes)—to exploit "reform and reopening" and to diffuse the benefits of growth? And how have Anxi farmers and businesspeople responded to changes in the local policy environment and in the larger Fujian economy? This chapter examines Anxi's response to the opportunities of the early post-Mao era.

A. Changes in Institutions and Policies

Reform. The most fundamental change in China since the late 1970s has been the implementation of reforms that reduce direct governmental intervention in the economy, allow much greater scope for private enterprise, and shift the locus of governmental activity toward the locale (rather than the center). While higher levels of government have continued to impose sometimes irksome constraints upon county decision-makers and upon farmers and other businessmen, there can be no doubt that the post-Mao years have seen a tremendous devolution of authority and the beginnings of a civil law to protect the rights being devolved.

In Anxi as elsewhere in rural China, early elements of institutional reform, such as decollectivization, produced an immediate motivational kick and a marked jump in agricultural output. Countywide, real GVAO increased by over 60 percent between 1978 and 1984.[1] Beyond these immediate effects, the reforms soon set in motion far-reaching changes in the organizational structure of the local economy, as farmers rushed to establish new enterprises and to shift surplus household labor from the fields into non-farm pursuits. By the mid 1980s, Anxi already had 18,000 specialized households, 2800 business partnerships, and almost 3400 registered private merchants—all forms of business unknown a few years earlier.[2] By 1990, private businesses accounted for 44 percent of retail sales in Anxi. Also by 1990, small-scale "township and village enterprises," operated by private owners, village cooperatives, and township governments, accounted for over 26 percent of the county's output—and constituted one of the most dynamic sectors of the local economy.[3] While no county-level data are available, it is safe to assert on the basis of provincial reports that these enterprises purchase the bulk of their inputs, and market their products, on the open market, essentially unburdened by the planning system. The Anxi government actively promoted development of such market-oriented businesses, through favorable treatment by the industrial/commercial bureau (e.g., in licensing), through assistance provided by various other local agencies, and through investment in marketplaces and other commercial infrastructure.[4]

In the early 1990s, the focus of rural reform in Anxi seems to have swung from decollectivizing agriculture and restoring markets to bringing some semblance of order and discipline to village finance and setting up "village cooperative funds" and other mechanisms for strengthening collective undertakings. Reports of 1991 and 1992 also point to campaigns to restructure county-run enterprises and reorganize local government.[5]

Regional Strategy. The institutional reforms at the heart of the post-Mao program were accompanied by sweeping policy changes, at all levels of government. In particular, the central government articulated a set of regional strategies premised upon differences in endowment and comparative advantage—including the widely publicized "coastal strategy" of the later 1980s. Taking their cue from the center, provinces formulated development strategies differentiating among their own internal subregions.

In the case of Fujian, in the early 1980s the provincial Communist Party Committee initiated a campaign to develop neglected mountain and ocean resources (*nian shan-hai jing*). This campaign evolved, by 1985, into a "two-front" strategy (the two fronts being the coast and the mountains of the interior), which laid out in broad outline different development plans for the two fronts. Fujian's regional strategy has since been elaborated in increasing detail, in terms of natural economic regions and urban growth poles for each, agricultural zones (such as those noted in Chapter 1), "belts" for designated industries, and specialized production "bases" for particular commodities. The provincial press has popularized development models suitable for each region—such as the "Jianyang model," based upon grain and forest products, for northwestern Fujian and the "Jinjiang model," based upon export-oriented and labor-intensive manufacturing, for the southeastern coast.

Regionally differentiated development strategies have entailed, of course, a turn away from the precept of regional self-sufficiency that characterized Maoist policy. Differentiation clearly presumes specialization and interregional trade, and implicitly endorses the sorts of reallocation that one might expect marketization (noted earlier) to precipitate. Abandonment of extreme self-sufficiency and reinvigoration of domestic commerce have been particularly important for Anxi: the county's principal products—notably teas, fruits, and handicrafts—can now be readily marketed outside the county. Indeed, specialized wholesale markets for such products emerged in Fujian in the mid 1980s, and national and provincial policies promoted development of this commerce by explicitly prioritizing consumer-goods production and endorsing increased personal consumption.

Restoration of the grain trade, coupled with a surge in national grain output, allowed Anxi to rely more heavily upon external food supplies. Fujian province dramatically increased its grain inflows from other parts of China, and also designated seventeen counties, all in the west of the province, as "grain bases." These bases—like the favored grain-producing areas of the 1960s and 1970s—receive preferential access to fertilizer and other inputs as well as injections of provincial investment funds for farmland capital construction. In return, they are required to supply a large flow of grain to the rest of the province. Hence, grain-deficit counties, like Anxi, are under much less pressure to increase their own grain output. A private grain trade, centered largely in the town of Guanqiao in Nanan county (bordering Anxi), handles a substantial portion of the west-to-east grain flow within Fujian.[6]

As shown in Figure 1.2 above, after the abandonment of grain self-sufficiency, grain output per capita in Anxi dropped markedly, to a low of 161 kilograms in 1986. Output per capita remained below 200 kilograms each year through 1992. The estimates in Figure 3.1, based upon reported output and plausible assumptions concerning consumption per capita, suggest deficits of about 90,000 tons per year in the late 1980s and early 1990s, as compared to 34,000 tons per year in the late 1970s.[7] This increase reflects an intentional shift of resources out of grain production into

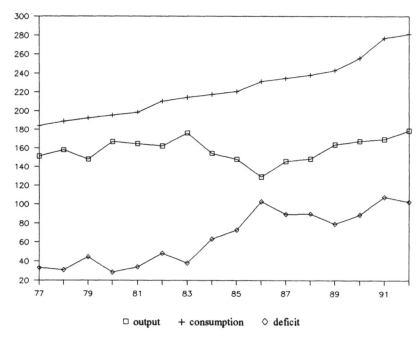

Figure 3.1. Anxi's Grain Deficit, 1977-92

Note. In thousands of tons, unhusked. Output in 1981 interpolated. Consumption and deficit estimated, assuming consumption (in all uses) of 270 kilograms per capita during 1977-80, 280 during 1982-85, 290 during 1986-90, and 300 during 1991-92. A supply of 270-300 kilograms per capita is generally viewed as adequate.

Sources. Tables A1, A5, and A7.

other crops and into non-crop activities, rather than a failing battle to produce adequate grain supplies locally.[8]

In terms of the coastal/interior distinction at the core of Fujian's regional policies, Anxi is officially cast as a coastal county (as elaborated in the next subsection). The eastern part of Anxi is in fact oriented toward Quanzhou and Xiamen, and toward its own dense overseas network. On the other hand, Anxi is geographically interior: Fengcheng, at the eastern edge of the county, is 58 kilometers from the coast at Quanzhou, by road. The western reaches of the county are oriented, by virtue of the mining and forest industries, toward Sanming and the heavy industrial belt of interior Fujian. And portions of the county have benefitted from "mountain-area" policies aimed at the interior; these policies, implemented by the provincial government in the wake of the *shan-hai* campaign, are mainly intended to stimulate development in poor mountain villages by intensifying exploitation of mineral and forest resources and by attracting capital and skilled manpower.[9]

Opening Up. Fujian province, along with neighboring Guangdong, pioneered post-Mao China's reopening to the outside world. Fujian is home to one of the first four Special Economic Zones (SEZs), and the province as a whole has enjoyed, since 1979, an array of "special policies and flexible measures" affording provincial and local authorities considerable latitude in dealing with foreign trading partners and foreign investors. Since 1988, Fujian (along with Guangdong and Hainan) has also been designated an "experimental area for comprehensive reform and opening up."

Fujian has aggressively courted foreign investors, especially overseas Chinese and, more recently, Taiwanese. Indeed, the provincial government has promulgated a series of special regulations for Taiwan-invested enterprises, intended to ensure protection of the investors' property and legal rights. Coastal cities have established enterprise zones specifically for Taiwan investors; Xiamen, for example, established the Haicang and Xinlin Investment Districts, and built power plants and other infrastructure to serve them.[10] Taiwan investment in Fujian took off in 1988, with 180 projects approved during that year, and $143 million (US) of Taiwan capital committed. By the end of 1991, Fujian had 1203 Taiwan-invested enterprises, with $1.6 billion committed.[11]

Fujian has also courted tourists. Destinations such as the Wuyi mountain district, historic areas of Quanzhou, and religious sites at Mazu and Quanzhou are widely publicized and easily accessible, and substantial investments have been made in the hospitality industry (hotels; restaurants; welcome stations; local, inter-city, and international transport). Efforts to attract Taiwanese visitors were greatly facilitated by the decision of the Taiwan government, in 1987, to relax restrictions on travel to the mainland, which loosed a flood of Taiwanese tourists. Some 16,000 visited Fujian in 1987, over 146,000 in 1988, and well over 200,000 each year thereafter.[12]

Although Fujian's reopening to foreign businesses did not affect Anxi as quickly and forcefully as it did the more developed coastal areas, Anxi certainly benefitted. With the rapid development of Xiamen after 1980, new demands for labor, raw materials and exportables, opportunities for subcontracting, and access to potential foreign investors began to spill beyond Tongan and Longhai, to more distant counties such as Anxi. Anxi began to engage in processing of materials under contract in the early 1980s, and received its first foreign investment in 1984. In 1985, Anxi was included in the newly-established Minnan [Southern Fujian] Open Area,

Table 3.1. Foreign Economic Relations, 1978-92

	1978	1984	1985	1986	1987	1988	1989	1990	1991	1992
Processing under Contract[a]										
number of contracts		10[c]	44	29		32	14			2
value[b]		0.275		5.434		0.488[d]	0.333[e]			
Foreign Direct Investment										
projects approved, cumulative		1	6	7	8	15	29	42	49	67
foreign-invested enterprises		0	4	4	6	7	16	26	32	
foreign investment newly approved[f]			1.060			0.980	3.3342			15.96
actual foreign investment[f]		0.215[g]	0.375[g]	0.425[g]	0.382	1.040	1.759	1.893	1.206	
Foreign Trade										
procurement by trade companies[h]	7.41	11.568	14.51	17.086						
procurement of export commodities[i]				29.3	26.56	27.07	24.02	28.04	39.25	49.52
exports of foreign-invested enterprises[f]				3.88	10.78	19.535	21.2016	10.72[j]		22.49

Table 3.1, continued

	1978	1984	1985	1986	1987	1988	1989	1990	1991	1992
production of industrial exports[k]							6.368	11.074	12.56	16.111
Tourism and Remittances										
tourist arrivals				1114			>3800[l]		>4500[l]	
remittances from abroad						≈10[m]	>10[n]	>20[o]	31.51	

Note: All values in terms of million current yuan unless otherwise indicated.

a. *Sanlai yibu.*

b. Million Hong Kong dollars.

c. For garments.

d. For 12 orders completed by year-end.

e. For 11 orders completed by year-end.

f. Million US dollars.

g. Converted from yuan, at the official exchange rate.

h. *Waimao shougou zongzhi,* at planned prices.

i. *Waimao chukou shangpin shougou zong'e.*

j. January through June only; up 23.3 percent over the same period of 1989.

k. *Chukou chanpin chanzhi, duli hesuan gongye qiye,* 1980 constant yuan; except 1993, *chukou jiaohuo zhi, duli hesuan gongye qiye,* current yuan.

l. Overseas Chinese and Taiwanese.

m. 1937 and 1988, sum.

n. For public welfare projects.

o. For schools.

Table 3.1, continued

Sources. For processing contracts: Minnan85, p. 124; Zhang and Lu, p. 579; FJJJNJ87, pp. 634-35; FJJJNJ89, p. 535; Huang, p. 259; FJJJNJ93, p. 459. For FDI: Minnan85, p. 124; FJJJNJ87, pp. 534-35; FJJJNJ88, pp. 94, 517; FJJJNJ89, p. 538; FJJJNJ90, p. 466; FJJJNJ91, p. 455; FJJJNJ92, p. 441; Huang, p. 259; FJJJNJ93, p. 459. For export procurement: Zhang and Lu, p. 579; FJJJNJ87, pp. 634-35; FJTJNJ87, p. 347; FJJJNJ88, p. 517; FJJJNJ89, p. 538; FJJJNJ91, p. 441; FJJJNJ92, p. 455; FJJJNJ93, p. 459. For FIE exports: FJJJNJ87, p. 635; FJJJNJ88, p. 517; FJJJNJ89, p. 538; FJJJNJ90, p. 465; FJRB, 10 August 1990, p. 2; FJJJNJ93, p. 459. For industrial exports: FJGYTJ91, p. 290; FJTJNJ92, p. 501; FJTJNJ93, p. 465. For tourists, FJTJNJ87, p. 347; FJJJNJ90, p. 466; FJRB, 2 February 1992, p. 7; FJJJNJ93, p. 459. For remittances, FJJJNJ90, p. 466; FJJJNJ91, p. 339; ZGNYNJ91, p. 120; FJJJNJ92, p. 441; FJRB, 21 February 1991, p. 3.

which encompassed eleven counties and cities in Jinjiang, Longxi, and Xiamen prefectures.[13] The Open Area (extended in 1988 to include 33 counties and urban districts) has enjoyed an array of preferential measures, such as remission of import duties on equipment and some current inputs and reduced tax rates on foreign-invested enterprises. In 1986 and 1987, three towns in Anxi—Hutou, Guanqiao, and Jiandou—were included among the "keypoint satellite industrial bases" designated by the provincial government—apparently in an attempt to concentrate industrial development, economize on social overhead capital, and foster linkages with Xiamen and other large cities.[14]

The influx of tourists who have come by the shipload to Xiamen and then dispersed to their ancestral homes has also been a boon to Anxi. The tourist trade brings not only transitory bursts of local spending and of giftgiving within the families reunited, but also prospects for business deals, ongoing remittances, and large-scale philanthropy.

The data collected in Table 3.1 measure some effects of Fujian's reopening upon Anxi. The first set of data (in the first two rows) suggests that processing of materials supplied by foreign customers peaked around 1986, at about 30 contracts, worth on the order of $700,000 (US) per year. The second set shows that, after a slow start, foreign investment in Anxi accelerated in the late 1980s and reached a cumulative total of about $7.3 million (US) by the end of 1991, when 32 foreign-invested firms were in operation. The third set shows exports growing rapidly and almost continuously, to over $25 million (US) per year by the late 1980s—reflecting export-promotion measures and liberalization of the foreign trade regime, as well as the activities of foreign-invested firms (many of which are engaged mainly in producing for export).[15] The final set (in the last two rows) shows tourist arrivals reaching about 4000 per year by the late 1980s, with the ready accessibility of the county as part of the Minnan Open

Area and with the flow of Taiwanese visitors into Fujian, and donations (including donations for schools and the like) reaching 20 million yuan per year by 1990, again reflecting the restoration of ties with relatives in Taiwan and overseas. Anxi ranks among the top six counties in Fujian, in terms of charitable contributions received.[16]

Overall, Table 3.1 points to a clear departure from the isolation that Anxi experienced during the Maoist era. The pace of change in Anxi, however, pales by comparison with those in the Minnan Open Area as a whole and in other counties of the Area. By 1991, for example, the entire Open Area already had 1200 foreign-invested enterprises; in 1991, enterprises and governments in the Area signed 846 contracts involving direct foreign investment, and actually brought in $322 million in foreign capital.[17] Anxi claimed less than 1 percent of these totals. As of 1986, Jinjiang county already had 40 foreign-invested enterprises in operation, as compared to Anxi's 4; in 1991, Jinjiang had 518, as compared to Anxi's 32.[18]

B. Fighting Poverty

National and Provincial Anti-Poverty Campaigns. As reform and reopening progressed, China's leadership became increasingly concerned with the possibility of widening income differentials and, especially, with the fate of locales and households at the bottom of the income distribution.[19] In 1985, China launched an anti-poverty campaign, intended to solve, by 1990, the problems of basic subsistence for at least 90 percent of the people living in poverty-stricken areas nationwide. About 300 counties were designated as national poverty "keypoints"—Anxi and thirteen other counties in Fujian among them. The central government extended low-interest loans to the keypoint counties, totalling about 1 billion yuan per year. It also allocated grain and other commodities to support infrastructure projects; these allocations, valued at 2.7 billion yuan nationwide for 1985-87, were used in lieu of cash to pay workers or were monetized by the provincial governments for purchase of construction materials.

In response to the central initiative of 1985, the Fujian government organized a provincial anti-poverty campaign, focusing on the fourteen national keypoint counties, plus three additional poverty counties and about 200 poverty townships designated by the provincial government itself. The principal goals of the provincial campaign were formalized as "3/5/8": solving the basic-needs problem for the great majority of poor households within *three* years (1986 through 1988), solving the problem of local budget deficits within *five* years, and enabling poor areas to make a positive contribution to the provincial economy (and in particular, to remit revenues to the provincial government) within *eight* years. To attain these goals, the province promulgated an anti-poverty strategy with four key components:

(1) investment in human capital—addressing the problems of deficient education, illiteracy, and lack of technical and business skills; ensuring that every poor household acquires technical expertise in at least one line of agricultural or handicraft production;

(2) commercialization—"developing commodity production" (i.e., production of goods for sale); bringing every poor household into the market economy, by diversifying family farms and introducing exportable cash crops, assisting with start-up of small non-farm businesses, and providing commercial services and market information;

(3) restructuring of village economies—correcting past misallocation and ecological degradation, and more fully exploiting local resources; transferring surplus labor out of agriculture and into local industry, commerce, and services; upgrading the local export base, with more value added (e.g., selling canned foods rather than unprocessed mushrooms, or furniture rather than lumber);

(4) cost effectiveness—orienting development assistance toward infrastructure and directly-productive projects that use local resources, require relatively small investments, yield quick returns, admit participation by large numbers of poor households, and stimulate further investment through backward or forward linkages.

To implement its strategy, the Fujian government created an anti-poverty bureaucracy. A new provincial leading group for economic development of poor areas is responsible for overall organization and coordination of poverty work provincewide. A provincial poverty-work office promulgates anti-poverty policy, conducts inspections of poverty work, and audits anti-poverty spending. Provincial anti-poverty work teams carry the campaign directly into townships and villages, with each team assigned to a poor area to implement provincial policies, run demonstration projects, and assist local leaders in formulating development plans. Various provincial-level agencies—apart from supplying personnel for work teams—are supposed to assist in the campaign by conducting surveys and studies in their own fields of expertise, dispatching technical specialists to take up temporary posts in poor-area schools and to train villagers in practical skills, and setting up long-term "direct links" with poor areas (through which they participate regularly in local planning and in project design and implementation).

With the launching of the central and provincial campaigns, spending intended to alleviate poverty increased dramatically, exceeding 1.3 billion yuan provincewide over the five years 1986 through 1990. By way of comparison, this is about 6 percent of all government budgetary expenditure in Fujian over the same period and about 400 yuan on average for each person in poverty-stricken households. Funding came from a number of sources:

(1) the central program of low-interest loans to poor counties—about 40 million yuan annually to Fujian during 1986-90;

(2) the central program of in-kind grants—over 9.2 million yuan to Fujian in 1990—used mainly to build roads and potable water systems;

(3) central assistance for Fujian's old-base areas and ethnic minorities—about 20 million yuan annually;

(4) a provincial fund of 100 million yuan for "supporting the economic development of poor areas" during 1986-88 (later expanded, and extended through 1990), to be used for education, investment in infrastructure, and interest-free loans for productive projects;

(5) prefectural and county-level "development funds," supported from local revenues;

(6) funds raised by local economic collectives and non-governmental organizations through voluntary contributions and local levies, and used to make loans and grants for household projects and small village projects.

In addition to its allocations earmarked for poverty work, the provincial government introduced a number of preferential measures for poor areas—48 such measures in 1985 and 19 more in 1986. In general, these measures were intended to provide greater local autonomy in economic decision-making, increase locally retained budgetary revenues, and improve the investment environment (so as to attract investment from richer areas). The 67 preferential measures were worth on the order of 100 million yuan per year to the designated poverty counties and townships.

The Campaign in Anxi. Anxi was, of course, very much involved in the anti-poverty campaign, as one of the designated poverty keypoints.[20] The county's attack on poverty was conceptualized as the confluence of three policies already announced by the center and province: (1) development assistance, in the forms of capital and technical and commercial knowhow, for poverty-stricken villages; (2) preferential measures for mountain-area development, to promote better use of abundant forest resources; and (3) the reopening to trade and investment. These three strands are repeatedly intertwined in the rhetoric of the county campaign. Hence, in 1987, the Anxi government stated that its efforts would focus upon external economic relations and "poverty work," and a published report emphasizes linking up with the outside as the basic means of escaping backwardness. A 1991 news item notes that "only when Anxi's mountain areas are developed will the people of Anxi escape poverty for good" and that "depending upon mountain resources and developing mountain areas provides Anxi with a path out of poverty."[21] Such general notions took on a more articulated form, as local surveys provided a detailed picture of local resources, the extent of environmental damage, and the magnitudes of the county's surplus labor problem and potential grain deficit. Around 1987, the county government and county CCP committee summarized their rural development strategy (somewhat awkwardly) as "taking grain as the foundation and forests as the base, using teas for escaping poverty, and fruits for becoming prosperous."[22] By the early 1990s, this had become a "strategy for escaping from poverty and for overall development,"

> focusing on lands still waiting to be opened;
> with the slogan 'tea to escape poverty and fruits to seek prosperity';
> calling upon farmers countywide to mount an attack on undeveloped mountain areas, with 'each household planting one mu of fruit, and each village 100 mu';

where forests are most appropriate, do forestry; where tea is most appropriate, plant tea; and where fruits are most appropriate, plant fruits.[23]

Of course, such rhetoric is not always translated into action. In the case of Anxi, however, tracing the county's development efforts does point to real emphases on creating new income streams through "developmental" agriculture (opening tea farms, fruit orchards and commercial forests, mainly in upland areas) and also through small-scale nonagricultural enterprises, and on attracting inflows of capital and skills, promoting export of local products, and modernizing grain farming. (See Section C, below.)

Organizationally, the anti-poverty campaign in Anxi replicates the framework implemented at the provincial level. The county set up its own poverty leading group and poverty office, and set forth an inspirational "guiding principle" for poverty work: "County, townships, villages, and the people—together we will prosper!" The county also formulated annual targets for the campaign; the 1987 target, for example, was 31,600—that is, 31,600 households were to escape poverty, by attaining incomes of at least 200 yuan per capita. Leaders at the county and township levels each developed "contact points" (county leaders with poor townships, township leaders with poor villages), and reportedly signed contracts taking overall responsibility for solving practical problems in their assigned locales and for implementing the various preferential policies intended to increase investment in poverty areas. Forty-odd county agencies sent people to take up posts in poverty-stricken villages and to assist in formulating local development plans. Village officials and party members were enlisted in anti-poverty responsibility systems, whereby each guaranteed to oversee implementation of anti-poverty plans and design of anti-poverty measures for certain households.[24]

Anxi, like other counties, formed its own anti-poverty work teams and accepted aid from teams formed by the province and prefecture. Work teams in Anxi reportedly assisted in setting up local enterprises, renovating and expanding existing enterprises, opening mines, developing mushroom and tree-ear production, upgrading low-yield tea farms, addressing erosion problems, starting fisheries, solving transport and input bottlenecks, and finding markets for local products. The Fuzhou railroad bureau, for example, sent a work team into Jiandou township to scout out marketable minerals and other local goods and to assist in transporting them.[25] By the late 1980s, poverty work was also being channeled through new "economic entities" [fupin jingji shiti]—generally, enterprises set up with anti-poverty funding, to employ people from poor households or to organize household

Table 3.2. County Budgetary Revenue and Expenditure, 1978-92

	Revenue[a] (1000 yuan)	Expenditure[a] (1000 yuan)	Subsidy[b]		
			total (1000 yuan)	per capita (yuan)	share[c] (percent)
1978	8080	8910[d]	830	1.2	9.3
1980	8547.4	13,332.1	4784.7	6.6	35.9
1983	9880	16,100	6220	8.1	38.6
1984	12,021.8	18,351.8	6330	8.1	34.5
1985	14,278	25,980[d]	11,702	14.9	45.0
1986	19,356	36,678[d]	17,322	21.7	47.2
1987	22,067	39,551[d]	17,484	21.6	44.2
1988	28,306	43,878	15,572	19.0	35.5
1989	33,403	49,837	16,434	19.6	33.0
1990	37,300	53,990	16,690	18.9	30.9
1991	44,730[e]	59,200	14,470	15.7	24.4
1992	53,320[e]	73,630	20,310	21.7	27.6

a. Budgetary only: excludes local extra-budgetary revenue and expenditure; current yuan.

b. Expenditure less revenue.

c. Share in expenditure.

d. Of which: 4,332 in 1978, for science and technology, education, culture, and public health, 11,893 in 1985, 14,500 in 1986, and 15,643 in 1987.

e. Of which: 38,600 from industrial and commercial taxes in 1991, and 45,300 in 1992.

Sources. Minnan85, p. 236; FJJJNJ87, pp. 634-35; FJJJNJ88, p. 517; FJJJNJ89, p. 538; FJJJNJ90, p. 658; FJJJNJ91, p. 664; FJJJNJ92, p. 614; FJJJNJ93, pp. 459, 693.

production around a center providing start-up loans and technical and business services.[26] And by the early 1990s, the sorts of work previously undertaken by "anti-poverty work teams" in Anxi seem to have fallen partly to "socialist education teams" sent into poor villages by provincial and county agencies.[27]

A breakdown of anti-poverty spending by locale and end use is not available. Anxi was fully eligible for the various sorts of anti-poverty funding, and the plight of the county, as one of the neediest in Fujian, was well-known to provincial authorities through household surveys. Hence, it is very likely that the inflow of resources to poverty-stricken areas of Anxi as a result of the poverty campaign amounted to several hundred yuan per capita during 1986-90, in line with the provincial average.

Data concerning the county budget shed some indirect light on just what the poverty campaign has meant to Anxi, in dollars and cents. As shown in Table 3.2, the provincial budgetary subsidy to Anxi (estimated as the difference between county expenditure and county revenue) jumped from 4.8 million yuan in 1980 to 17.3 million in 1986—nearly tripling in real terms.[28] Over half of the increase in the county's expenditure between 1980 and 1986 was financed by this jump in the subsidy. After peaking in 1987, the subsidy held fairly steady at around 16 million yuan per year during 1988-90—still well over 30 percent of expenditure.

In addition to inflows via the county budget, Anxi also received various forms of anti-poverty assistance directly from provincial bureaus; this assistance totalled almost 20 million yuan in 1986 and 1987 (the only years for which data are available).[29] And Anxi benefitted from many of the province's 67 preferential measures for poverty-stricken areas. For example, one such measure allowed Anxi's ten designated poverty townships to retain 50 percent of the revenues generated by taxes on bamboo and lumber products, rather than the 30 percent retained by other townships. Such measures directly increase local revenue, rather than increasing the provincial subsidy to Anxi.

The new bureaucracy and the funding devoted explicitly to poverty work were undoubtedly important in the attack on poverty within Anxi. More generally, the anti-poverty campaign required government employees and community leaders at all levels to acknowledge and address the problems of the poor—and may have instilled in some a genuine concern with the plight of the least fortunate. The campaign brought into Anxi planners, technicians, and businesspeople with skills of value in local development. And it forced the government of Anxi, for perhaps the first time, to produce a development strategy grounded in a thorough knowledge of local resources and current conditions.

C. Development Efforts

Anxi's development during the 1980s and early 1990s has been conditioned by the programs of reform and reopening and of poverty alleviation underway across Fujian and across China, and by guidelines laid out by the provincial and central governments. This section examines specifics of Anxi's development efforts, within this larger context.

Improving Production of Grain and Livestock. In the early 1980s, agricultural labor productivity in Anxi stood at about one-half the provincial average, in terms of both grain output per worker and GVAO per worker.[30] In part, this low productivity reflects excessive concentration upon grain production—lavish use of labor in grain fields, coupled with neglect of other activities. The post-Mao program entails a shift away from grain (as noted in Section A of this chapter); however, grain will remain a mainstay of the county economy for a long time to come, both because parts of the county are ideally suited to production of rice and sweet potatoes and because substantially greater dependence upon outside suppliers (as compared to the degree of dependence already reached) brings risks that county leaders are very reluctant to accept. Addressing the problem of low productivity also entails, then, efforts to improve the low yields on a significant portion of the county's grain land and to attain wider diffusion of superior techniques and inputs. A central component of the county's development program has in fact focused upon the grain branch, in conjunction with complementary farm activities.

The anti-poverty campaign in Anxi began with designation of the county as a "pilot project in escaping poverty through science and technology," in 1985.[31] The Fujian Academy of Agricultural Sciences selected Longmen township as a "science and technology anti-poverty demonstration site" and sent in teams of specialists to improve the crop and livestock branches and to develop suitable on-farm sideline activities. These teams undertook at least ten projects—in such areas as introducing improved varieties of rice, introducing non-traditional grains such as rye, improving erosion control, selecting better varieties of livestock (especially pigs), setting up stations to supply breeding stock, and developing mills to produce high-quality feed. One of the resultant farm-management regimes, based upon integrated production of grain, lean pork, and sidelines, reportedly increased household incomes by 160 percent over a four-year period. Another regime, based upon growing rye and raising geese, was designed to generate additional income during the winter slack season.[32]

Table 3.3. Cultivated Area, 1980-92

	Total Area (mu)	Paddy Fields (mu)	Dry Fields (mu)	Machine Plowed Area (mu)	Effectively Irrigated Area (mu)	Stable Yield Area[a] (mu)
1980	411,298	384,073 (93.4)[b]	27,225 (6.6)[b]	46,000 (11.2)[b]	228,000 (55.4)[b]	91,000 (22.1)[b]
1983	410,000	380,000 (92.7)	30,000 (7.3)			
1984	407,700	377,700 (92.6)	30,000 (7.4)		252,800 (62.0)	
1985	405,301	374,476 (92.4)	30,825 (7.6)	36,331 (9.0)	245,980 (60.7)	93,000 (22.9)
1986	403,500	372,000 (92.2)	31,000 (7.8)			
1987	400,500	368,800 (92.1)	31,700 (7.9)	48,000 (12.0)	246,000 (61.4)	
1988	399,000			44,000 (11.0)	253,000 (63.4)	
1989	398,147	364,531 (91.6)	33,616 (8.4)	60,200 (15.1)	254,100 (63.8)	183,000 (46.0)
1990	395,659	362,073 (91.5)	33,586 (8.5)	60,691 (15.3)	254,698 (64.4)	185,157 (46.8)
1991	394,500				253,500 (64.3)	
1992	393,000				255,000 (64.9)	

a. "Hanlao baoshou" (protected against both flood and drought, so as to ensure good harvests).

b. Figures in parentheses: share of total cultivated area, in percent.

Sources. ZGFXNC80-87, p. 205; ZGFXNC88, pp. 82, 84; Minnan85, p. 121; Zhang and Lu, pp. 573-74; Fujian cehui ju, following p. 36; FJJJNJ87, p. 633; FJNCTJ91, pp. 289, 291, 293, 325; FJTJNJ92, p. 495; FJTJNJ93, p. 459; unpublished data collected by Bruce Stone, International Food Policy Research Institute.

Table 3.4. Manufactured Inputs to Agriculture, 1980-92

	Agricultural Machinery				Village Use of Electricity (1000 kwh)	Chemical Fertilizers	
	total (kw)	large tractors[a]	small tractors[b]	irrigation equipment (kw)		actual weight (tons)	nutrient content (tons)
1980	27,949				15,820		6312
1983	30,700					50,469	9526
1984						58,711	12,142
1985	60,756	119	1949	2332	11,450	61,577	13,037
1986	72,100		>2000[c]			74,805	16,395
1987	82,539				16,724	84,433	18,856
1988	93,150				22,210		20,046
1989	96,921	43	3216	3140	25,710	108,230	24,433
1990	95,283	35	3071	3267	26,810	108,628	25,410
1991	98,506				36,950		28,246
1992	106,568				38,160		27,773

a. Large and medium tractors (over 20 horsepower).

b. Small tractors and 2-wheeled walking tractors.

c. Includes large and medium tractors.

Sources. ZGFXNC80-87, p. 205; ZGFXNC88, p. 85; Zhang and Lu, p. 574; Minnan86, p. 138; Minnan88, p. 154; FJJNJ87, p. 155; FJNCTJ91, pp. 305, 307, 323; FJTJNJ92, p. 495; FJTJNJ93, p. 459; unpublished data collected by Bruce Stone, International Food Policy Research Institute.

Similar projects were undertaken in other towns and townships, with the assistance of provincial and county agencies. A project in Jiandou, for example, was designed to overcome local skepticism about hybrids, by demonstrating new crop rotations tailored to local conditions and using hybrid rice, soy, and potatoes; grain output nearly doubled over a two-year period.[33] Other programs to improve grain production have included promotion of winter cropping, use of green manures, afforestation (to limit erosion and silting), restoration and maintenance of irrigation systems, upgrading of low- and medium-yield fields, establishment of township erosion-control stations, attempts to concentrate grain fields in holdings of optimal size and in the hands of the most capable farmers, and more vigorous efforts to popularize improved varieties.[34] Especially since 1986 (after the area sown to grain plummeted), the county has tried to tighten land management, with efforts at recovering superior farmland alienated for non-farm uses and establishment of "arable land management districts" for monitoring land use.[35] County agencies have also launched campaigns designed to increase use of modern inputs and to sustain funding for use of such inputs during periods of financial strain.[36] In the wake of farmer complaints about the fertilizer distribution system, in 1991 the Anxi Supply and Marketing Cooperative tripled the number of fertilizer outlets county-wide and substantially improved inventory control and delivery services.[37] Reports of the early 1990s suggest further attention to the livestock sector, through introduction of superior types of cattle and pigs, establishment of breeding stations, opening of experimental pastureland "bases" for the cattle industry, and development of better feeding regimens.[38]

Anxi appears to have made a considerable effort to popularize technical changes in grain and livestock farming, once their effectiveness is proven. The provincial press reported in some detail both the specific regimes developed at Longmen and elsewhere in the county and the general campaigns for modernization and improved farm management. The regimes in Longmen were also popularized by conducting training classes for farmers and local officials throughout Anxi and by bringing people from poverty areas to the demonstration sites.[39] The county established a science commission, a network of science associations, and various institutes for research in the agricultural sciences, and sent technical experts to serve as "vice mayors" in poverty townships.[40] Although no specifics are available, it is very likely that Anxi developed the three-tier extension system typical of Fujian counties—with county-run agencies, including an extension center, overseeing technical-service stations with full-time technicians at the township level and part-time extension workers in villages.[41] County reports do mention "technical demonstration farms"

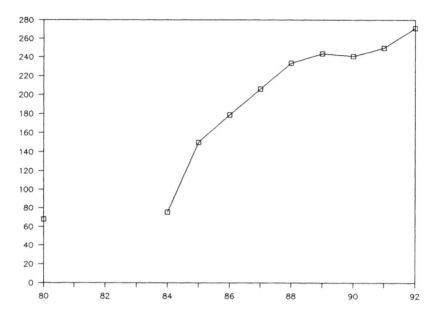

Figure 3.2. Agricultural Machinery, 1980-92

Note. In watts per mu cultivated.

Sources. See Tables 3.3 and 3.4.

(i.e., farms that serve as models for their villages) and county-organized training classes for demonstration farmers.[42]

Declines in Anxi's effectively irrigated and the machine-plowed areas during the mid 1980s probably resulted in part from decollectivization and the subsequent neglect and mismanagement of collective property and from the decisions of cost-conscious farmers faced with surplus household labor.[43] (See Table 3.3.) After 1987, the irrigated area recovered—and surpassed—the level of 1984, as village administrations were consolidated and responsibilities assigned, and as the county and provincial governments organized restoration efforts. The machine-plowed area recovered at about the same time, surpassing earlier levels by 1989. These increases in irrigated and machine-plowed area occurred despite a gradual decline in cultivated area that continued throughout the 1980s. In fact, the decline in cultivated area in Anxi is much less pronounced than that for the province or for other counties in Jinjiang prefecture; the cultivated area of the prefecture as a whole declined by 7.2 percent, and that of Jinjiang county (including the city of Shishi) by 12 percent, between 1980 and 1990—as

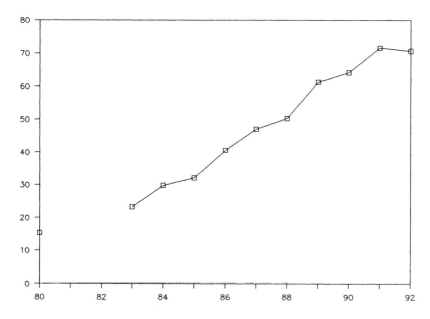

Figure 3.3. Application of Chemical Fertilizers, 1980-92

Note. In kilograms of nutrient per mu cultivated.

Sources. See Tables 3.3 and 3.4.

compared to 3.8 percent in Anxi.[44] As shown in the table, in Anxi a decrease in paddy-field area was partially offset by an increase in dry fields.

As shown in Table 3.4, Anxi's stock of farm machinery (measured in terms of motive power) more than tripled between 1984 and 1990.[45] By 1992, Anxi had 271 watts of machinery per mu cultivated (Figure 3.2), as compared to 350 for Fujian as a whole.[46] Interesting, the number of large and medium tractors in Anxi dropped off steeply, once farmers were allowed to make their own investment decisions—whereas the number of small and two-wheeled tractors increased by over 50 percent between 1985 and 1990. With the increase in the stock of farm machinery on hand, consumption of electric power (and undoubtedly of other forms of energy) increased apace.

Table 3.4 also shows that application of chemical fertilizers doubled between 1980 and 1985, and doubled again between 1985 and 1991. By 1992, Anxi used about 71 kilograms of chemical fertilizers per mu cultivated (Figure 3.3), as compared to 50 in Fujian as a whole. The Fujian level exceeds the national averages of all but a few countries.[47]

With the greater use of modern inputs and farming methods, the grain yield in Anxi increased by 13 percent between 1980 and 1992; this increase served to offset a decline in the area sown to grain, resulting in a modest increase in total output.[48] Attention to grain production and complementary activities also served to contain overt unemployment, by reducing the exodus of farm people searching for non-farm jobs. Such jobs, although on the increase, still absorbed only a small portion of the county's rural labor force throughout the 1980s (as shown in Chapter 4).

Village Restructuring and Commercialization. Consistent with provincial guidelines, economic policy in Anxi became increasingly outward-oriented during the 1980s. The county government began actively promoting local products throughout Fujian, across China, and abroad, and it assisted adjustments in the composition of village output and the development of local "bases" for production of marketable goods. Various county agencies were called upon to improve provision of commercial services and technical support for cash-crop farming and for non-farm enterprises.[49]

While grain continues to claim the bulk of Anxi's farmland and, therefore, to limit production of commercial crops that compete directly with grain, the county has large areas of hilly land suitable for tree crops and forest-based industries.[50] In keeping with the *shan-hai* and mountain-area strategies then being promulgated, in the early 1980s Anxi's commercialization efforts focused largely upon such activities. Although gestation periods are relatively long, initial investments in, e.g., tree crops can be made largely in the form of farmland capital construction, using surplus household labor. Incomes and tax revenues eventually derived from the output then support construction of processing capacity as well as welfare programs and other local expenditures.

The county first pursued village restructuring and commercialization by encouraging individual households to specialize, via preferential measures aimed at farmers willing to enter contracts for production of particular commodities.[51] By the later 1980s, the county had shifted toward promoting villagewide specialization in primary products, local processing of such products in village enterprises, and development of related services by both private ventures and local collectives. This approach was popularized in the policy of "one product per village, one industry per township," with each village basing its choice of specialty on local resources and traditional skills. In the case of Shangqing township, for example, each of seventeen villages is said to have specialized in a particular "cornerstone product" (such as longan, in Zaokeng village), with the township itself developing its own "leading industry" (bamboo- and rattan-processing).[52] While it is unlikely that Anxi villages generally adhered to the arbitrary "one-product" stipulation, instances of village-level commercialization, via introduction of new product lines, are very widely reported in the local press.

In some areas of the county, commercialization has been promoted through "anti-poverty economic entities" that support production and marketing of particular goods, and through construction of "export-commodity bases," where production is geared to world market demand as reflected in the local procurement activities of foreign-trade companies.[53] Teas and fruits have remained the principal candidates for commercial production; other products frequently promoted in recent years include mushrooms and tree ears, traditional medicines, pine rosin and related products, bamboo, and—beyond tree crops and forest products—fish, ducks, pottery, and flagstone.

Tea is Anxi's most important agricultural specialty. Across the county, more than sixty varieties are grown—among them, Tieguanyin and Huangjingui, which are highly regarded throughout China and abroad. During the 1980s, the county organized a campaign to address the problem of low yields (noted earlier), through farmland capital construction projects on 60,000 mu of existing tea fields, through popularization of superior tea varieties, and through training programs for tea farmers.[54] And, with the restoration of markets and government efforts to encourage cash-crop production, tea area increased rapidly (Table A6).

Tea-processing capacity in Anxi was also increased, accommodating the greater supply of tea leaves. Older plants, such as the state-run Anxi Tea Factory in Guanqiao, the Lutian Township Tea Factory, and the Xiping Township Tea Factory were expanded and modernized; Anxi Tea, for example, employed 2201 in 1989, up from 1459 four years earlier.[55] Apart from the larger plants, which process mainly teas of export quality, over 50 village-run plants were operating by 1987, and several hundred by the early 1990s.[56] The county set up a "Wulong Tea Research Institute" and a "Wulong Tea Quality Control Center" and instituted inspection and sampling procedures. It also began to market local teas aggressively, by advertising in Shanghai and other cities, participating in national and international exhibitions, opening sales outlets in cities nationwide, and exporting via Shantou, a traditional center of the tea trade (and now a Special Economic Zone).[57] For Anxi Tea Factory alone, exports amount-ed to 22 million yuan in 1990; since Lutian, Xiping, and other plants also export, the county's total exports certainly ran much higher.[58]

Fruit production seems to have suffered more serious neglect during the Maoist era than did tea, and has made a more rapid post-Mao comeback. The Anxi government called for each village to plant a collective orchard of 100 mu and for each household to maintain a private orchard of 1 mu, and it promulgated a set of preferential policies for specialized fruit farmers.[59] Large plots in hilly areas of the county have been leased to individuals and partnerships for long terms, specifically for growing fruit trees.[60] (Such leasing is common in Fujian). The county's annual reports mention substantial areas newly planted to fruits each year—almost 22,500 mu in 1989, and 82,200 mu in 1992.[61] Cultivation of exportables, in particular, has spread widely; the Anxi persimmon, a well-known local specialty, spread from a small area in Chengxiang and Fengcheng to at least seven other towns and townships.[62] In addition to new plantings of fruit orchards, over 20,000 mu of existing low-yield orchards were "transformed" through measures to improve soil quality and to provide for water control.[63]

As noted earlier, efforts were launched during the 1980s to conserve forests, increase forested area, and develop forest-based products. The Anxi government promulgated a responsibility system for forestland (i.e., leasing out of forestland for private management), and organized seeding of extensive areas from the air and large campaigns for plantings by teams of workers on the ground.[64] The most widely noted forest products of recent years are mushrooms and other edible fungi. Because these products do not demand large initial investments or require long gestation periods, they are viewed as excellent income generators for poor villages in forested areas. The Anxi Supply and Marketing Cooperative has supported such efforts, by opening an "edible fungi development center" and initiating extension services for mushroom growers.[65] Production has boomed in many parts of the county. Lantian township, for example, set up a mushroom "production base." Longjuan township invested one million yuan in mushroom production, bringing in expertise from Gutian county, the leading mushroom producer in Fujian; local income reportedly increased by 12 million yuan per year as a result of this project.[66]

Production of mushrooms, like teas and many fruits, has strong forward linkages to processing industries and the export trade. Much the same is true of bamboo, which is also widely produced in Anxi. During the 1980s, the county experienced a modest boom in township and village enterprises (TVEs—locally owned, non-agricultural businesses, typically of small size), many of which engage in processing of agricultural outputs. Countywide, the number of TVEs in operation, the number of workers employed in them, and the income they generated appear to have increased quite rapidly through 1988 (as shown in Table 3.5). Then, under the national policies of retrenchment, employment remained more or less constant in 1989—and real output and income fell.[67] Growth resumed in 1990, and accelerated through 1992; during the spring of that year, new TVEs were opening at the rate of about nine per day.[68] The data in Table 3.5 pertain to TVEs in all sectors; industry, however, predominates. Apart from processing of agricultural outputs, Anxi's TVEs also produce substantial quantities of building materials, chemicals and products thereof, coal, and consumer goods such as garments and shoes.[69] Most of the TVEs in Anxi are privately operated (i.e., *not* township- and village-operated, in the table).

Despite the growth reflected in Table 3.5, Anxi remains relatively backward, in terms of the size of the TVE sector and its level of sophistication. As of 1991, each of Anxi's TVEs employed only five workers and generated only 26,000 yuan of gross income, on average. Many TVE employees are part-timers who also work in agriculture, and many are illiterate and unskilled.[70] Through 1989, only eleven TVEs were export-oriented enterprises.[71] By way of comparison, Jinjiang county—a provincial model of TVE-driven development—had twice as many enterprises, and each enterprise, on average, employed twice as many workers and generated over three times as much income.[72]

Anxi's relative backwardness in terms of TVEs has been ascribed to the low level of development in the county (and, hence, deficiencies in infrastructure and input supply) and to a disadvantageous location (compared to, e.g., coastal Jinjiang). But the county government also cites misdirection of TVE investment, lack of indigenous "backbone" enterprises that can provide technical and business leadership for small TVEs, failure to develop distinguished products and to establish a reputation for quality and value, an inability to move from handicraft production of traditional goods to factory production of more upscale items, and deleterious competition among Anxi firms in pursuit of outside customers.[73] Beginning around 1988, the county launched a more vigorous effort to guide TVE development, promulgating separate "models" for eastern and western Anxi. The western model, based upon Gande township, centers on exploiting mineral and energy resources; the eastern model, based upon the experience of Hutou, centers on consumer goods, such as garments and plastic items. As retrenchment caused losses and increasing debt in 1989, the county tried to assist TVEs—and, in particular, to attract outside expertise and capital and to diffuse more fully the technical and marketing knowledge introduced into Anxi by foreign-invested enterprises. As of 1990, seven foreign-invested TVEs were in operation.[74]

Table 3.5. Township and Village Enterprises, 1984-92

	1984	1985	1986	1987	1988	1989	1990	1991	1992
Number of enterprises	4134	5524		8640		6355[a]	7069	8000	9455
township- and village-operated		1079				984	1004		
Employment				32,874	35,000	35,493	37,304	39,846	51,555
township- and village-operated		26,281				20,265	19,048		
Gross output (million yuan)			116.14	141.74	186.55	187.96	213.13	284.55	569.88
Gross income (million yuan)	61.45	90.5		139.06	182	189.15	211.04	293.18	57.124
township- and village-operated						113.82	123.91		
Taxes paid (million yuan)				6.57	7	9.22	11.16	15.35	24.22
Profit (million yuan)			10.71	11.91		12.7	13.97		
Exports (million yuan)					6.6	14			

Table 3.5, continued

Note: All values in current prices. TVEs (township and village enterprises) include sole proprietorships, partnerships, and other privately owned businesses, as well as those operated by townships and villages. See also Tables 4.7 and A9.

a. Possible change in coverage, between 1987 and 1989.

Sources. For 1984-87: Minnan85, p. 122; Minnan86, p. 137; FJJJNJ87, p. 634; FJJJNJ88, p. 516; FJRB, 6 December 1988, p. 2; FJJJ, April 1989, p. 22; FJNCTJ91, pp. 16, 18, 257. For 1988: FJTJNJ89, p. 517; FJJJNJ89, p. 537; Huang, p. 260. For 1989-91: Huang, p. 260; FJJJNJ90, p. 465; FJTJNJ90, pp. 492-93; FJJJNJ91, p. 455; FJNCTJ91, pp. 16, 18, 257; FJTJNJ91, p. 485; FJTJNJ92, p. 497; FJTJNJ93, p. 461.

The county also organized efforts to market local products, by sponsoring exhibitions, in Hong Kong, of goods produced by TVEs, setting up sales outlets in Guangdong, Hainan, and elsewhere in China, and providing specialized training for officials involved in foreign trade. Several local products—including Wulong tea (as noted earlier), textiles and garments, umbrellas, machinery, porcelainware, and handicrafts—were accorded priority for export promotion.[75]

With the push to commercialize during the 1980s, many villages seized upon TVEs as a quick solution to their poverty problems and a means of absorbing surplus labor made conspicuous by the new household farming regime.[76] Some villages—those advantageously located, those with entrepreneurial and well-connected leaders—undoubtedly prospered. For most, however, commercialization probably meant a process of trial-and-error and gradual discovery of a few activities yielding modest increases in local incomes. For example, in Zhuanwen, a poverty-stricken village in Chengxiang township, early efforts to commercialize included a transport venture using the village's tractors, a construction company to market the services of Zhuanwen carpenters, training of seamstresses to work in nearby foreign-invested enterprises, a workshop that employed local women to produce bamboo- and rattanware, and development of persimmon farming.[77]

By the early 1990s, development of the collective economy was becoming an increasingly conspicuous element of Anxi's development policy. As noted in Table 3.5, about 1000 of the TVEs in Anxi were operated by townships and villages as of 1990; in addition, many villages operated collective orchards or tea plantations. The essence of the collective, though, appears to be substantially different from that of the Maoist era. The village collective is now more a business entity, which invests in promising enterprises in various sectors, markets their products aggressively, and uses the profits to provide social overhead; it is no longer a social entity overseeing virtually all aspects of its members' lives.[78] The collective is also being called upon to provide services (often on a fee-for-service basis) and to assemble and disseminate the information (about markets, technical innovations, input supplies) that is essential for success in increasingly competitive businesses.

Unsurprisingly, Anxi has experienced an increase in the degree of commercialization, as a result of policies aimed at development of commercial, rather than subsistence, activities. The rural "commodity rate" (purchases from the agricultural sector, as a share of GVAO) jumped from 33 percent in 1985 to 66 percent by 1990. As shown in Table 3.1, procurement of export commodities within the county exceeded 39 million yuan in 1991, roughly three times the level of 1978 (in nominal terms).[79] And, although modest by comparison with coastal counties, TVE exports did reach some 14 million yuan by the late 1980s—up from virtually zero a few years earlier (Table 3.5).

Attracting Capital and Knowhow. By the late 1980s, county leaders viewed outside investment as an integral part of Anxi's rural anti-poverty strategy, as well as a means of spurring the industrialization of Fengcheng (the county seat) and other towns.[80] Anxi began to compete with—and to emulate—other locales, in order to attract investors. The county government formulated "ten preferential measures for foreign-invested enterprises and enterprises with domestic partners" to supplement the provincial measures already in place for the entire Minnan Open Area, streamlined administrative procedures for foreign-invested enterprises and, as noted earlier, tried to appeal to the kinship and native-place loyalties of Hong Kong and Taiwan businesspeople with ties to the county. In 1989 or so, Anxi formulated priorities for outside investment during the 1990s, according highest priority to projects in infrastructure, basic industries, export-oriented agriculture, and general agricultural development.[81] Given the backward state of the Anxi economy (and the scarcity of capital and skills, in particular) and the competition among counties for investment, however, it is unlikely that Anxi is turning away willing investors whose preferred projects rank low on the government's list.

Apart from various special inducements, the appeal of Anxi is rooted mainly in its surplus of cheap labor—and, for certain industries, its natural resources, local specialties, and traditional skills. In Anxi (and in other, similarly endowed counties), technologies that are no longer competitive in the high-wage economies of Hong Kong and Taiwan can be profitably resuscitated, and outdated equipment kept in service.

Table 3.6. Foreign-Invested Enterprises, by Branch and Size, 1991

Branch[a]	Registered Capital (1000 USD)					
	<200	200-400	400-600	>600	not reported	all
Food products	1					1
Beverages		1		1		2
Textiles		2				2
Apparel	5	5	3		1	14
Furniture	1		1			1
Arts and crafts	2		1			3
Chemicals	1	3				4
Rubber products	2					2
Plastics		1				1
Metal products		3				3
Machine building	1		1			2
Transport equipment	1					1
Sectors other than industry	1			1		2
All	14	15	6	2	1	38

a. For 25 of the 36 industrial enterprises, assignment to a branch is explicit in a Chinese source; for 8 more, the branches are evident from the names of the enterprises. The questionable cases are included in metal products (2) and textiles (1).

Source. Table A8.

Table 3.6 summarizes the structure of the foreign-invested sector in Anxi. Of 38 FIEs (foreign-invested enterprises) identified, the garment industry has the largest share, by number of enterprises, with 14; other industries with three or more enterprises include metal products (umbrellas), arts and crafts (rattanware, silk flowers), and chemicals (recording tapes, and personal care products such as shampoo). Beyond these, foreign investment is scattered thinly across a number of other industries producing simple consumer goods. In terms of location, most FIEs are headquartered in the county seat of Fengcheng, but again there is a scattering of enterprises in Hutou, Penglai, Kuidou, Xiping, Jingu, and Shangqing.

Of the 38 enterprises represented in Table 3.6, 25 are equity joint ventures *(hezi qiye)*, two are cooperative ventures *(hezuo qiye)* and eleven are wholly foreign-owned. Regardless of the form of the venture, FIEs in Anxi are generally quite small. As shown in the table, only eight (of 37) enterprises have registered capital of $400,000 (US) or more, and none approaches $1 million. The mean for all 37 is about $276,000. Most of the foreign investment in Anxi has come from Hong Kong—with, in some cases, Hong Kong intermediaries investing Taiwan money. As of 1989, Taiwan investors owned equity in at least two ventures. In that year, an agreement involving $3 million (US) in Taiwan capital was signed, for quarrying of granite in the town of Guanqiao (a venture not reflected in Table 3.6). New Taiwan investment committed to Anxi totalled $3.12 million (US) during the first half of 1990—and there has undoubtedly been substantially more since then.[82] As of 1992, county reports noted signs of a shift toward larger foreign investment projects, in such industries as cement.[83]

The Anxing group and the Fenghua Garment Company are among the most important FIEs in Anxi. The Anxing Rattan Company, a joint venture between a county-run handicraft enterprise and a Hong Kong investor, was established in April 1984—the first FIE in the county. It grew rapidly, to about 4600 employees by the end of 1986 and to 6753 by the end of 1987. As of late 1991, Anxing employed over 7200 workers, in 62 processing workshops throughout the county. Local sourcing of inputs and services creates additional employment and income. The company markets furniture, baskets, and other bamboo and rattan products in North America, Europe, and Australia—to customers in over 20 countries. In 1989, Anxing established two additional ventures, to produce silk flowers and garments.[84] Fenghua (or Frank Well) Garment is a joint venture between two Anxi companies, a provincial import/export company, and a Hong Kong investor. Employment increased from 35 at startup in 1986 to 2028 by mid 1992, as Fenghua became Fujian's largest producer of athletic apparel. Like Anxing, Fenghua markets worldwide; product lines are continually updated, and sales efforts are shifted in response to changing world-market conditions. In the early 1990s, for example, the company focused on new markets in Eastern Europe, the Middle East, and Africa. Fenghua also sells domestically, through outlets in 50-odd cities across China.[85]

Both Anxing and Fenghua have had substantial impact upon poverty-stricken areas of Anxi. As of late 1988, some 48 of Anxing's workshops were located in such areas, with over 5000 employees drawn from poverty-stricken households. The company's workshop in poverty-stricken Zhongshan village (Shangqing township), for example, created jobs for members of 250 (out of 410) households, increasing average household income by over 1200 yuan.[86] Fenghua is also specifically cited for its contributions toward alleviating poverty; the company has seven processing workshops in poverty townships.[87]

Anxing, in particular, provides a striking example of employment creation through foreign investment. But Anxing is not unique: Table 3.6 indicates that much of the foreign investment in Anxi has sought out labor-intensive industries using relatively simple technologies in small-scale workshops. Investment of this sort creates jobs with modest skill requirements—and with minimal commitments of local capital. As noted earlier, such investment may also have substantial spread effects, especially in those cases where techniques are easy to replicate and where locally available raw materials are suitable as inputs. By 1990, Anxi's foreign-invested enterprises employed over 10,000 workers, with a wage bill well in excess of 20 million yuan—and they created additional employment for suppliers of inputs and services.[88] FIE exports totalled over $20 million per year (as noted in Table 3.1, above), and FIEs paid 16 million yuan in taxes.[89]

In addition to the labor-intensive industrial enterprises listed in Table 3.6, Anxi has also attracted foreign investment in real estate development and in agriculture. The Sandexing project in Fengcheng, undertaken by an overseas Chinese investor, entails construction of a residential and commercial complex of 14,000 square meters.[90] Taiwan entrepreneurs had invested heavily in at least four "developmental agriculture" projects by mid 1992, with several more under discussion. One of these projects, the Anxi County Agricultural Development Company, rented township-owned tea land and brought in modern farming and management methods from Taiwan.[91]

The investment data in Tables 3.1 and 3.6 certainly do not capture the entire flow of foreign capital into Anxi. In some cases, kinsmen overseas donate substantial sums earmarked for investment projects that are then undertaken by residents of the county. This appears to be true for at least some of the projects financed by the famous "Mr. Li," whose contributions to the development of fruit production in poverty-stricken areas are widely reported in the provincial press.[92] It is probably also true in the town of Penglai, which in 1990 claimed eleven enterprises—in such industries as plastics, garments, and tea-processing—that had been set up with capital from overseas kinsmen.[93] The Anxi government and the governments of towns and townships throughout the county have pursued such contributions, by honoring donors at public ceremonies, producing

Table 3.7. Investment in Fixed Assets, 1980-92

	Total	BCC Completed[a]	State, BCC[a] total	State, BCC[a] productive[b]	State, Renovation[c]	State, Other	Urban Collective	Urban Private	Rural Private
1980			16.83		6.92[d]		0.38		
1981-82[e]			25.25						
1983			17.13		2.67		0.17		
1984			23.42		3.99		0.36		
1985			28.87	24.16	5.46		1.78		
1986			28.83	24.86	5.13		1.41		
1987	84.59	35.80[f]	29.13	24.02	12.22	2.74	5.93	6.77	19.75
1988	77.60	32.43[f]	21.19	17.97	9.29		8.11		
1989	56.96	35.76[f]	22.66		6.63				
1990	92.22	26.18[f]	14.32	6.66	8.61		0.78		
1991			9.13	1.30	7.85		1.22		
1992			13.19	4.69	22.53				

Note: All values in millions of current yuan.

Table 3.7, continued

a. Basic capital construction.

b. Investment in productive assets, such as factories (as opposed to, e.g., housing).

c. Replacing equipment and otherwise updating existing capacity.

d. As given in source; may be a typographical error, for 0.692.

e. Sum of two years.

f. Precise coverage uncertain.

Sources. For 1987: YHJJKF, pp. 442-43; Minnan87, p. 184. For Column 2 (except 1987): FJJJNJ88, p. 729; FJTJNJ89, p. 524; FJTJNJ90, p. 498; FJTJNJ91, p. 494. For all other data: Zhang and Lu, p. 585; Minnan85, pp. 222-24; Minnan86, p. 139; Minnan87, p. 184; FJJJNJ87, pp. 634-35; Minnan88, p. 169; Fujian shehui kexue yuan, p. 18; FJJJNJ90, p. 465; FJTJNJ90, p. 499; FJJJNJ91, p. 455; Minnan92, p. 209; FJTJNJ92, pp. 507, 509; FJTJNJ93, pp. 471, 473.

promotional materials such as videotapes, and cooperating with native-place societies abroad (notably, the Anxi Guild of Singapore).[94]

Anxi's wooing of outside capital was intended to attract investment from other areas of Fujian, as well as from other countries. In attempting to attract domestic investment, Anxi was able to exploit a provincial campaign promoting "horizontal economic and technical cooperation" during the mid and late 1980s.[95] For example, enterprises in Jinjiang county, where local industry is relatively developed, were encouraged to establish "big sister" links with Anxi, opening branch factories in the county and supplying credit, technology, and market information.[96] In 1989, fifteen "mountain/coastal joint enterprises" opened in Anxi; by mid 1991, 57 were in operation, with total investment of 14 million yuan. These are apparently ventures in which companies from prosperous coastal areas (including some outside Fujian) invest in Anxi enterprises or provide technical assistance, in exchange for access to raw materials and cheap labor.[97] The governments of Anxi county and Jinjiang prefecture also organized efforts to place workers from Anxi in jobs in Quanzhou, Shishi and Jinjiang county, and in Xiamen.[98] The extent of such "horizontal cooperation" and its impact upon the Anxi economy are not clear in published sources.

Apart from cooperation with coastal areas, in 1988 Anxi also entered into a joint venture with Sanming Steel, the largest steel mill in Fujian. The joint venture, the San-An Company, produces iron, ferrosilicon, and ferromanganese alloys in Anxi, by bringing capital and technology from Sanming and exploiting local mineral resources and hydro potential. Output is supplied to the Sanming mill.[99]

State-Funded Investment. Apart from formulating general policies and attempting to implement both its own policies and those of higher levels through the various measures already described, the Anxi government has invested in social overhead capital and in "backbone" enterprises owned and operated by various county bureaus. Much of this state investment has been linked explicitly to "improving the investment environment," by providing decent transportation and communications, a better-educated workforce, and adequate supplies of electricity, water, and basic materials such as cement, bricks, and lumber.[100]

Table 3.7 collects data on investment in fixed assets within Anxi. State investment in basic capital construction (BCC) nearly doubled between 1980 and 1987 (in nominal terms), and then fell off, probably due to the retrenchment initiated in late 1988 and the resulting funding problems. BCC investment during the three peak years, 1985-87, is roughly the same, in nominal terms, as BCC investment during 1949-78 inclusive.[101] Investment in technical renovations follows a time path similar to that of BCC, with a sharper climb to the 1987 peak, and with a second sharp upswing in 1992.

State-funded BCC has been directed mainly toward transportation and communication systems and toward electric power stations and transmission lines. The largest and most important project is construction of the Zhangping-Quanzhou rail line, 115 kilometers of which lie in Anxi. This project, initiated in 1979, has entailed a total investment of well over 100 million yuan. Other major projects of the 1980s include construction of the Xianghua-Longjuan highway, the Nanmen Bridge (in Fengcheng), and a new telecommunications building; reconstruction of the Hutou-Jiandou highway; installation of a modern telephone switching system and a number of new inter-township telephone lines; and construction of the Cunnei 3200-kilowatt power plant (completed in the early 1980s), the Jianan and Yuantan power plants, and a 110-kilovolt transmission line from Hutou to Quanzhou, to link Anxi with the provincial power grid.[102] Projects of the early 1990s include upgrading and construction of intercounty highways connecting Anxi with Nanan, Quanzhou and Tongan, and construction of the 25-megawatt Lantian Hydroelectric Plant.

Apart from major state-funded projects, a substantial amount of investment in infrastructure—village roads, feeder canals for irrigation, potable water systems, and small hydroelectric stations—is undertaken by individual farmers and by rural collectives, or is financed by overseas Chinese. This is apparently included in "rural private investment in fixed assets" in Table 3.7—although the extent to which scattered small projects are reported remains open to question. Various central and provincial

programs aimed at supporting infrastructure projects in poor and mountain-
ous areas may also have brought investment resources into the county, in
addition to those reported in the table.[103]

With these investments by government and other agents, the state of
Anxi's infrastructure improved considerably during the 1980s.[104] The
western section of the Zhangping-Quanzhou line was completed by 1985,
connecting the town of Jiandou to Xiamen via Zhangping and the Ying-Xia
line—and providing the county with its first rail service. The section from
Jiandou to the village of Changji (in western Bailai) was laid in 1988, and
that from Changji to Hutou in mid 1992. As of 1992, Anxi's road network
measured 1485 kilometers—double the total of 1978; the major roads
linking Fengcheng with other population centers had been paved, and over
90 percent of the villages in the county were accessible by motor vehicle.
Scheduled bus service connected Fengcheng with Xiamen, Quanzhou, and
other major cities in Fujian. By 1992, Anxi had 3290 telephones (up from
1825 just two years earlier); prior to the upgrading and expansion of
telephone service, placing long-distance calls from rural areas had
sometimes involved waits of several hours, undermining efforts to attract
investors. The county generates over 100 million kilowatt-hours of electric
power from small hydroelectric stations—one of only twelve counties in
Fujian to do so.[105]

In the mid 1980s, the Anxi government began to formulate a plan for
developing the towns of Fengcheng (the county seat) and Hutou—and for
investment zones, apparently intended to attract Taiwan investors. As of
1992, county plans called for an enterprise zone centered on Fengcheng,
designed to exploit links with foreign-invested businesses and with overseas
kinsmen, and including strips along the major roads intersecting at
Fengcheng. As part of this scheme, the urban district of Fengcheng was
expanded from under 1 square kilometer to about 4.8, and the county began
to invest in improving streets, the Xi River embankment, and public utilities
such as water service. A number of new commercial and industrial sites
were made available for lease.[106] The county also began to address a
growing urban housing problem, with investment in new construction and
with a housing-reform program for sale of existing state-owned housing
units.[107]

A significant portion of the total investment in fixed assets has been
directed toward education and health care. And, as they did 50 years ago,
Anxi's overseas kinsmen have made substantial contributions in these
spheres; in recent cases reported in the provincial press, one overseas
Chinese family donated some 10 million yuan for a pre-school, an
elementary school, a middle school, and a vocational school, another family

donated 8 million yuan for a middle school on an 86-mu campus, and yet another donated $10 million (HK) for a hospital. Other, less spectacular, cases are frequently reported.[108] Countywide, the number of elementary and middle schools increased from 411 in 1984 to 466 in 1991, and many existing school buildings were renovated (some having fallen into such disrepair that they posed serious safety hazards to students). The number of hospital beds in the county increased from 601 to 713 over the same period.[109] Apart from investment in fixed assets, the county's current budgetary expenditures on "science, education, culture, and health care" increased quite rapidly during the 1980s—from 4.3 million yuan in 1978 to 15.6 million in 1987.[110] Much of this increase, however, probably reflects substitution of state-funded services for those previously provided under the commune regime. A portion of the increase also reflects a rebuilding of local capacity for research (e.g., in agricultural sciences) and for technical education. By the later 1980s, Anxi was reporting significant numbers of technical research projects, some of which earned provincial and national recognition.[111]

Government investment in factories and mines seems to have focused largely upon technical renovations, rather than BCC.[112] The mid-80s boom in renovation expenditures (Table 3.7) reflects a county policy of emphasizing improvement of existing capacity over new construction (and may also reflect some disguising of new construction as renovation, in order to skirt administrative restrictions).[113] Dozens of technical renovation projects have been noted in county reports; the major state-owned factories (in, e.g., the tea processing, building materials, metallurgical, and chemical industries) have all been expanded, modernized, and equipped with new production lines. The state-owned portion of Anxi's industrial sector, however, remains relatively small—and county policy toward industry has clearly emphasized TVEs and foreign-invested enterprises. As of 1990, the county had only 28 state-owned industrial enterprises with independent accounts, with a total of 50-odd state-owned enterprises engaged in industry.

D. Summary and Concluding Comments

Reform and opening up, and the vitality of the larger South China economy, suddenly created a realm of opportunities unavailable to Anxi during the 1960s and '70s. The evidence surveyed in this chapter shows that the Anxi government, and local farmers and businesspeople, responded with considerable alacrity to these new opportunities. The county formulated and implemented, for example, a number of measures intended specifically to exploit its membership in an "Open Area," its designation as a "poverty keypoint," and its status as the ancestral homeland of many overseas Chinese. Local policies appear to have become increasingly attuned to local resource endowment and local shortages—promoting employment of surplus labor, cultivation of tree crops in the county's hill country, and importation of capital and of technical and business skills from other areas of the province and from abroad. The Anxi government appears to have defined for itself a new, supportive role, through investment in social overhead capital and maintenance of a policy environment congenial to private enterprise. Local farmers shifted out of subsistence agriculture, plunged into novel market-oriented activities, and sent their children to work in new off-farm businesses. A new class of entrepreneurs began to emerge—on export-oriented farms, in the larger industrial TVEs, in the retail and service industries, and especially in and around the foreign-invested sector. By 1990 or so, these responses to reform and opening up had coalesced into a coherent strategy focused upon:

—modernizing the core of Anxi's agriculture (grain, pigs, and poultry);

—diffusing other agricultural activities (teas, fruits, mush-rooms, fisheries) and rural non-farm enterprise, and hence new income streams accessible to the majority of Anxi households;

—aggressively pursuing foreign investment in labor-intensive and export-oriented industries;

—accumulating the physical infrastructure and human capital needed to support the growth of commercial agriculture, of domestic non-farm enterprises, and of foreign-invested firms.

Notes

1. See Table A2.

2. These are respectively *zhuanye hu* (specialized households, which derive most of their incomes from a single product, and market the bulk of their output

thereof), *lianheti* (business partnerships), and *shangye geti hu* (private merchants). Data pertain to 1985. FJJJNJ87, p, 634; Minnan85, p. 124.

3. FJSYTJ86-90, pp. 128, 130; FJTJNJ91, pp. 467, 485; ratio of TVE gross output to social gross value, both in current prices. Township and village enterprises (TVEs) are locally owned and operated, either by township and village collectives or by private partnerships and individuals.

4. E.g., FJRB, 15 May 1988, p. 2; FJRB, 29 April 1990, p. 2; FJJJNJ88, p. 516.

5. FJRB, 7 July 1991, p. 2; FJRB, 13 August 1991, p. 1; FJJJNJ93, p. 459.

6. Lyons 1993, pp. 719-20.

7. Although the precise time path of Anxi's grain deficit may differ from that suggested in Figure 3.1, there can be no doubt that the deficit increased markedly. Even with no increase at all in consumption per capita, the deficit would have doubled over the period in question as a result of a decrease in output per capita and an increase in population.

8. See Sections B and C below, for further elaboration.

9. E.g., FJJJNJ86, pp. 653-60.

10. On regulations for Taiwan investors, e.g., FJJJNJ91, pp. 676-79, and FJJJNJ92, p. 660; see also FJJJNJ89, pp. 55-56. On investment zones, e.g., CD, 25 June 1990, p. B3, and FJRB, 14 October 1990, p. 1.

11. FJJJNJ89, p. 55; FJJJNJ92, p. 186.

12. FJTJNJ92, p. 346.

13. The city of Xiamen (which was already an SEZ) is not included in the total of eleven opened in 1985.

14. FJJJNJ88, p. 94.

15. The export figure in the text is the sum of two items in the table: exports from foreign-invested enterprises and exports of commodities procured by the foreign-trade companies. As the data in the table suggest, a consistent series

of export data is not readily available. The data in the table, however, leave no doubt that a substantial growth in foreign trade has occurred.

16. The ranking pertains to 1990; FJRB, 28 March 1991, p. 1.

17. Minnan92, p. 11.

18. FJTJNJ87, p. 348; FJJJNJ92, p. 439.

19. This subsection is based on Lyons, 1992b.

20. In fact, Anxi is also a revolutionary base area (as part of the An-Nan-Yong Soviet of the 1930s) and has a small minority population—and is therefore eligible for continuing assistance under older programs targeting "base areas" and minority areas.

21. These examples are from FJJJNJ88, p. 517; Chen and Chen; and FJRB, 25 April 1991, p. 4.

22. Huang, p. 255.

23. FJRB, 25 April 1991, p. 4.

24. FJJJ, August 1988, pp. 28-29; FJJJNJ88, p. 517; see also Lyons, 1992b.

25. E.g., FJJJNJ87, pp. 22, 69; FJRB, 5 April 1987, p. 1; FJRB, 6 December 1988, p. 2; see also FJRB, 15 November 1990, p. 2.

26. FJJJNJ88, p. 518; FJJJNJ90, p. 466.

27. FJRB, 12 May 1992, p. 4; FJRB, 17 May 1992, p. 2; FJRB, 10 June 1992, p. 2.

28. The real increase is obtained by applying the provincial retail price index, from FJTJNJ92, p. 314.

29. FJJJ, November 1988, p. 30; FJJJNJ88, p. 518.

30. This claim appears in FJJJNJ86, p. 654; it is consistent with Anxi data for 1980 and 1984, as collected in Tables A1, A2, and A7, and the Fujian data in FJFJ, pp. 36, 40, 41.

31. FJJJNJ86, p. 154.

32. FJRB, 2 September 1987, p. 2; FJRB, 8 January 1988, p. 1; FJRB, 19 April 1988, p. 1; FJRB, 3 February 1990, p. 2.

33. FJRB, 21 December 1988, p. 2.

34. E.g., Huang, p. 256; FJRB, 10 November 1987, p. 2; FJRB, 5 December 1988, p. 1.

35. E.g., FJRB, 4 August 1990, p. 2. The land-management districts in Anxi are modeled on those in Huian county; on Huian, see FJRB, 9 December 1990, p. 2.

36. E.g., FJRB, 29 January 1989, p. 2.

37. FJRB, 16 March 1992, p. 2; FJRB, 10 April 1992, p. 1.

38. FJRB, 30 April 1992, p. 3; FJRB, 8 June 1992. p. 6; FJRB, 8 October 1992, p. 6. See also FJJJ, August 1988, p. 28.

39. FJRB, 2 September 1987, p. 2.

40. FJJJNJ87, p. 635.

41. For a description of the three-tier system in Fuqing county, see FJRB, 12 August 1991, p. 1; see also FJNYDQ, pp. 518-20, and FJNCTJ91, p. 11. In the late 1980s, technical assistance was increasingly provided on a fee-for-service or contract basis, with extension workers responsible for generating revenue to cover a portion of their stations' operating expenses.

42. E.g., FJRB, 11 July 1992, p. 1; FJRB, 17 July 1992, p. 8.

43. For comments on irrigation during the 1980s, see Stone, pp. 312-23, and Nickum.

44. ZGFXNC80-87, 204-05; FJTJNJ91, p. 483. It should be noted that the cultivated area data are subject to a substantial margin of error; see, e.g., Crook.

45. The shares of inputs used for grain cannot by isolated; the data in the table pertain to county totals, for all farm uses.

46. Fujian data from FJTJNJ93, pp. 173, 175.

47. Fujian data from FJTJNJ93, pp. 173, 176; international comparison based upon World Bank 1993, pp. 244-45.

48. Anxi's yield increase (output per mu sown to grain) is smaller than those in Jinjiang prefecture as a whole (27 kilograms per mu sown, or 11.0 percent), and in Fujian province (38 kilograms per mu sown, or 15 percent) between 1980 and 1991; ZGFXNC80-87, pp. 204-06; FJTJNJ92, pp. 99, 492, 494. For further comment, see Chapter 4.

49. For general comment on Anxi's outward orientation, see Chen and Chen, pp. 163-68; see also FJJJNJ88, p. 517.

50. As of the mid 1980s, about 900,000 mu suitable for forestry, fruit- and tea-growing, and livestock grazing were not being used; FJJJ, November 1988, p. 29.

51. Huang, p. 257.

52. FJJJ, November 1988, p. 31; FJJJNJ91, p. 455.

53. As noted in Section B, "anti-poverty economic entities" are usually centers that arrange loans, supply services, and retain technicians to advise specialized producers; e.g., FJJJNJ90, 466. Export-commodity base construction is noted in, e.g., FJJJNJ88, p. 517.

54. FJJJNJ87, p. 636; Huang, p. 256; FJRB, 21 May 1992, p. 6.

55. FJJJNJ87, p. 831; ZGQYGK, p. 354; Zhang, Shao, and Gao, p. 167.

56. FJJJNJ88, p. 118; Huang, p .256; FJJJNJ93, p. 459.

57. Zhang and Lu, p. 582; FJRB, 18 January 1989, p. 2; FJRB, 23 May 1991, p. 2; FJRB, 5 January 1992, p. 5; FJRB, 9 January 1992, p. 2; FJJJNJ93, p. 459.

58. FJJJNJ91, p. 152; FJJJNJ92, p. 145; see also FJJJNJ89, pp. 59, 539; Huang, p. 256.

59. Huang, p. 257; FJJJ, November 1988, p. 31; FJJJNJ93, p. 458.

60. E.g., FJRB, 30 August 1991, p. 2.

61. FJJJNJ91, p. 455; FJJJNJ93, p. 458. See also Table A6.

62. FJNYKJ, April 1988, p. 35.

63. Huang, p. 257; the figure pertains to 1985-89.

64. Huang, p. 256.

65. FJRB, 16 March 1992, p. 2.

66. FJRB, 6 December 1988, p. 2; FJRB, 10 June 1992, p. 2. Many other counties in Fujian have also plunged into the mushroom business, depressing prices and raising worries about renewed degradation of forest resources.

67. The inflation rate in 1989 was 19 percent; FJTJNJ92, p. 315.

68. FJRB, 22 June 1992, p. 2.

69. FJJJNJ88, p. 118.

70. FJJJ, April 1989, p. 23.

71. Huang, p. 262.

72. FJTJNJ90, p. 492.

73. This paragraph is based on Huang, pp. 263-64; and FJJJ, April 1989, pp. 22-23.

74. Huang, p. 260.

75. Huang, p. 265.

76. Shimen village, in Gande township, is a widely cited example, of TVE-driven growth and poverty alleviation; FJRB, 25 September 1987, p. 1; FJRB, 20 August 1987, p. 1.

77. FJRB, 5 January 1987, p. 3. This source focuses on a village-level Communist Party rectification, and the village cadres' acquiring a more liberal "commodity mentality" as a result.

78. For general comments on the nature of the collective, see Oi.

79. For agriculture: FJTJNJ87, p. 280; FJNCTJ91, pp. 27, 209; increase in exports derived by linking the growth rates of the first two export series in Table 3.1.

80. This paragraph is based on FJJJ, August 1988, p. 28; FJRB, 4 July 1990, p. 3; Huang, p. 259.

81. Huang, p. 265; Chen and Chen, p. 165.

82. Huang, p. 260; FJRB, 7 August 1990, p. 2.

83. FJRB, 28 June 1992, p. 8.

84. FJJJ, June 1987, p. 1; FJJJNJ88, p. 212; FJRB, 15 December 1988, p. 1; FJJJNJ89, p. 59; ZGNYNJ91, p. 120; FJRB, 20 September 1991, p. 2; FJJJNJ93, p. 799.

85. FJRB, 7 March 1991, p. 3; FJRB, 20 June 1991, p. 2; FJRB, 19 June 1992, p. 2; FJJJNJ93, p. 799.

86. FJJJ, June 1987, p. 1.

87. FJJJNJ90, p. 465; FJRB, 20 September 1991, p. 2.

88. Huang, p. 259; ZGNYNJ91, p. 120; FJWSTZ, pp. 166-98; FJRB, 4 July 1990, p. 3; FJRB, 20 September 1991, p. 2.

89. The tax figure pertains to 1989; FJRB, 4 July 1990, p. 3. Many FIEs still enjoyed tax holidays—part of the package of concessions implemented to attract them.

90. FJRB, 29 March 1992, p. 7.

91. FJRB, 6 May 1992, p. 6; FJRB, 28 June 1992, p. 8; FJRB, 12 July 1992, p. 6.

92. E.g., FJRB, 25 April 1991, p. 4; FJRB, 16 June 1992, p. 2; FJRB, 4 August 1992, p. 2.

93. FJRB, 12 October 1990, p. 2.

94. FJRB, 21 February 1991, p. 3; FJRB, 6 March 1992, p. 8; FJRB, 26 July 1992, p. 7. In October 1992, the Anxi Guild of Singapore convened the first World Congress of Anxi Kinsmen, with over 600 persons attending. The next meeting will be convened in Anxi; FJRB, 18 October 1992, p. 1.

95. E.g., FJJJNJ87, pp. 65-66; FJJJNJ90, pp. 61-62; FJJJ, March 1991, pp. 7-8.

96. FJJJ, August 1988, pp. 28-29; see also FJRB, 15 November 1986, p. 2; FJRB, 17 March 1992, p. 6.

97. Huang, p. 262; FJRB, 30 December 1990, p. 2; FJRB, 20 September 1991, p. 2.

98. FJRB, 5 June 1991, p. 3; FJRB, 11 May 1992, p. 2.

99. FJRB, 8 December 1990, p. 2; FJRB, 19 October 1992, p. 3.

100. E.g., FJRB, 3 February 1991, p. 2, notes total spending of over 200 million yuan on infrastructure, to improve the investment environment.

101. FJJJNJ87, p. 634; Fujian shehui kexue yuan, p. 18.

102. Minnan85, p. 123; Zhang and Lu, p. 577; Huang, pp. 257-58; FJJJNJ87, p. 832; FJJJNJ88, p. 516; FJJJNJ89, pp. 291, 537; FJJJNJ90, p. 465; FJJJNJ91, p. 455; FJRB, 24 March, 1992, p. 6; FJJJNJ93, pp. 247, 459.

103. In addition to the programs noted in Section B, Anxi has benefitted from a central program for rural electrification; see, e.g., FJJJNJ85, p. 130. For examples of overseas Chinese financing of road construction, see FJRB, 27 March 1991, p. 3, and FJRB, 19 January 1992, p. 5.

104. This paragraph is based upon Huang, p. 258; Zhang and Lu, p. 577; FJTJNJ91, p. 493; FJRB, 4 October 1992, p. 7; Minnan92, p. 209; FJTJNJ93, p. 469. Concerning the Zhang-Quan rail line, see FJJJNJ89, p. 291; and FJRB, 21 August 1992, p. 6.

105. The claim concerning electric power pertains to 1990; FJJJNJ91; pp. 136-37.

106. FJJJNJ88, p. 517; FJJJNJ89, p. 539; FJJJNJ90, p. 465; FJRB, 4 July 1990, p. 3; FJJJNJ92, p. 441; FJJJNJ93, p. 459.

107. FJRB, 21 April 1992, p. 4. State investment in BCC for housing is reported at 1.49 million yuan in 1990; FJTJNJ91, p. 494. Housing is included in "non-productive" BCC in Table 3.7.

108. The three cases described are from FJRB, 24 October 1990, p. 3; FJRB, 26 April 1992, p. 2; FJRB, 3 May 1992, p. 8. For others, see FJRB, 3 January 1991, p. 4; FJRB, 16 May 1991, p. 4; FJRB, 19 January 1992, p. 5. See also FJRB, 12 April 1992, p. 7.

109. Zhang and Lu, p. 580; FJJJNJ91, p. 455; FJJJNJ92, p. 441; FJTJNJ92, p. 516. Some of the improvement in educational and health-care facilities is attributable to philanthropic giving by overseas Chinese.

110. This is an average annual increase of 15.3 percent (in nominal terms)—as compared to 18.0 percent for the county's total budgetary expenditures. See Table 3.2, above.

111. FJJJNJ88, p. 517; FJJJNJ91, p. 455. What limited capacity Anxi had possessed was severely damaged during the Cultural Revolution, and did not begin to revive until 1978; Zhang and Lu, p. 582.

112. Total investment, for both BCC and renovation, in 18 state enterprises (those controlled by the county's economic commission) totalled 46.94 million yuan over the twelve years 1978-89; Huang, pp. 257-58.

113. The remainder of this paragraph is based upon FJJJNJ87, p. 634; Huang, pp. 257-58; FJJJNJ90, p. 465; FJJJNJ92, p. 441. Most of the state factories in Anxi are county-owned (rather than prefectural, provincial, or central); for further comment, see Chapter 4 and (for an explanation of independent accounting) Table 4.8.

4
The Post-Mao Era:
Results

The preceding chapters have shown that reform and reopening, and the local responses to them, brought Anxi unprecedented growth. This chapter examines the extent to which the county has experienced not just a burst of growth but also fundamental changes in economic structure and, hence, in the sources of growth and of improvements in local welfare.

A. Structural Change

Sectoral Composition of Output. Figure 4.1 shows GVIAO (Gross Value of Industrial and Agricultural Output) and its structure between 1978 and 1992.[1] The rapid growth of GVIAO, at an annual rate of over 11 percent, is apparent in the figure. So too is the change in composition, with the weight of industry—especially light industry—increasing markedly. As shown in Figure 4.2, 85 percent of the increment in GVIAO between 1978 and 1992 originates in industry. Only 12.4 percent of the 1978-92 increment originates in crops and livestock—as compared to 51.5 percent during 1950-78.[2] (The forestry and fishery branches of agriculture were too small to contribute a substantial portion of the increment during either period.)

GVIAO is a deficient indicator of aggregate output, in that it covers only two sectors and admits double-counting. Table 4.1 decomposes four superior indicators, for 1992 and, for two of the four, for 1985 as well. (See Chapter 2 for further explanation of the various indicators.)

Unfortunately, the indicators in Table 4.1 are given in current prices (with no county-level sectoral deflators available) and only for very recent years; hence, they are not very useful for detailed examination of structural

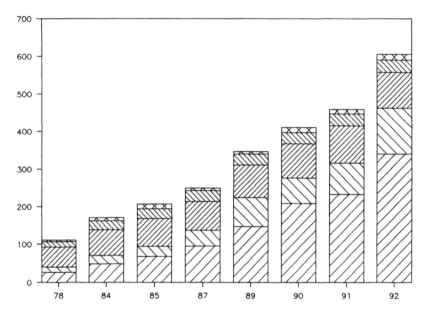

Figure 4.1. Components of GVIAO, 1978-92

Note. In millions of 1980 constant yuan. Components are, from bottom: light industry, heavy industry, crops, livestock, forestry and fisheries. All data in terms of "new" definitions (i.e., team and village enterprises included in the appropriate sectors, rather than in agriculture). Agricultural sidelines are excluded throughout. For 1978, livestock, forestry, and fishery components are assumed identical in new and old definitions. For 1991 and 1992, county deflators for components are applied to data in 1990 constant prices.

Sources. For 1978: FJJJNJ87, p. 634; Minnan85, pp. 207-12. For 1984: Zhang and Lu, pp. 574, 585. For 1985: Fujian shehui kexue yuan, p. 200; Minnan86, p. 137; FJJJNJ87, p. 634. For 1987: FJGYTJ88, pp. 308-09; Minnan87, p. 182. For 1989: FJTJNJ90, pp. 462, 481. For 1990: FJTJNJ91, pp. 478, 487. For 1991: FJNCTJ91, pp. 47-66; FJGYTJ91, pp. 268-69; FJTJNJ92, pp. 481, 490, 499. For 1992: FJTJNJ93, pp. 454, 463.

changes over time. Nevertheless, a few broad inferences can be drawn from the table. First, the four sets of data appear to be mutually consistent and based upon the same underlying set of accounts. Hence, netting out double-counting (moving from SGV to NMP) reduces the shares of industry and construction, which rely most heavily upon material inputs. The rural economy sees a larger share of total output originating in agriculture, and less in industry, than does the county as a whole. And the share of GDP originating in the tertiary sector is much larger than the share of SGV or NMP originating in transport and commerce, reflecting the broader coverage of services in GDP. Second, the shift into industry is, as

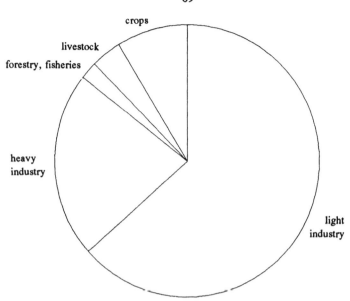

Figure 4.2. Components of GVIAO Increment, 1978-92

Note. In 1980 constant yuan. The components of GVIAO are as follows (in 1000 yuan):

	1978	1992
light industry	26,090	339,650
heavy industry	13,610	122,510
crops	52,940	95,750
livestock	13,980	32,181
forestry	4780	14,518
fisheries	40	580.

Sources. See Figure 4.1.

expected, quite pronounced: the industrial share of SGV, for example, jumps from about 30 percent in 1985 to over 50 percent by 1992. Interestingly, even in terms of GDP (which nets out the greater degree of double-counting in industry and accords greater weight to services), the secondary sector was already substantial as of 1985. The tertiary share was large, as well—and growing rapidly. Third, agriculture accounts for 40 percent of RSV in 1992—down from 66 percent in 1985, reflecting a rapid shift into industry and other non-agricultural sectors in the countryside, not just industrialization in the county's five towns.[3]

Table 4.1. Sectoral Components of Aggregate Output, 1985 and 1992

	SGV[a]		RSV[b]	NMP[c]	GDP[d]	
	1985	1992	1992	1992	1985	1992
Total	361.52	1368	897.5	576	210.41	701
agriculture	44.6%	26.2%	39.9%	42.9%		
industry	30.5%	51.4%	35.6%	34.4%		
construction	15.9%	14.8%	7.0%	12.2%		
transportation	3.5%	2.4%	5.2%	3.0%		
commerce	5.5%	5.2%	12.2%	7.6%		
primary					51.5%	35.1%
secondary					28.5%	37.8%
tertiary					20.0%	27.1%

Note: Values in million current yuan.

a. Social Gross Value.

b. Rural Social Value.

c. Net Material Product.

d. Gross Domestic Product.

Sources. Tables A3 and A4; Fujian shehui kexue yuan, pp. 22, 129; FJTJNJ93, pp. 443, 452.

Labor Force and Employment. Table 4.2 turns from output to labor input. The first line of the table shows that the total population of Anxi increased by some 26 percent during the 1980s—an average annual increase of slightly over 2 percent. The total increase is comparable to the reported natural increase alone, suggesting that Anxi has not experienced a large outmigration.[4] Unfortunately, the official population figures do not capture migrants who leave Anxi without transferring their household registrations. Significant numbers of Anxi residents have undoubtedly taken up jobs in Xiamen, where a boom in manufacturing and construction created a demand for labor that is now spilling beyond the neighboring counties of Tongan and Longhai. Such migration from Anxi has not attracted much comment in county reports, perhaps because to date the outflow has remained relatively modest.[5] The next three lines of the table pertain to the official classification of Anxi residents as agricultural or non-agricultural (the latter meaning registered in households entitled to subsidized grain rations from the state). As late as 1990, over 94 percent of the county's residents were classified as agricultural. Even among the 269,000 people resident in Anxi's five towns [zhen], some 86 percent belonged to agricultural households, since the boundaries of towns encompass substantial rural areas. The true urban population (as measured by the non-agricultural population in towns) numbered about 37,100 in 1990, up 38 percent over 1985.[6]

The participation rate in Anxi, measured as the ratio of reported labor force to total population, exceeded 39 percent during the 1985-90 period.[7] As shown in the second part of Table 4.2, the labor force is conventionally classified into three mutually-exclusive groups: village laborers, staff and workers (i.e., those employed by the state or by urban collective enterprises), and the urban self-employed. Village laborers account for the bulk of the labor force. Staff and workers totalled about 10 percent of the total in 1990, down from 15 percent in 1987—probably reflecting the retrenchment of the late 1980s and a campaign to streamline state organs. Staff and workers are mainly drawn from households classified as non-agricultural; most work in towns. The urban self-employed undoubtedly account for a larger share than the 0.3 percent indicated in the table, since many do not register their businesses and are therefore excluded—or, more likely, are counted as village workers.

Agriculture accounted for about 70 percent of the county labor force in 1987, and village non-agricultural employment for about 14 percent.[8] The corresponding shares for 1990 are 71 percent and 18.5 percent—these increases mirroring the decrease in "staff and workers."[9] In fact, the share of the labor force engaged in non-agricultural activities is probably understated somewhat throughout the table: each village worker is assigned to only one category, and those working part-time in off-farm jobs appear to be included in "agriculture." Table 4.2 suggests that services—transportation, commerce, and much of the "other" category—have played a conspicuous role in creating jobs; TVEs (discussed in Chapter 3) account for a substantial portion of the service-sector, as well as industrial, employment in Anxi's villages.

The last few lines Table 4.2 show that, as early as 1987, about 28 percent of the labor force was employed in the secondary and tertiary sectors. These workers produced almost 60 percent of Anxi's GDP, reflecting the substantially higher average labor productivity in non-agricultural activities.[10]

Table 4.2. Composition of Population and Labor Force, 1980-92

	1980	1985	1987	1990	1992
Population	728,628	792,766	814,141	916,204	943,900
agricultural	696,562	748,102	766,757	865,104	891,300
non-agricultural	32,066	44,664	47,384	51,100	52,600
in towns		26,944	29,618	37,100	46,900
Labor Force (1)	272,000	310,400	342,700	363,716	≈396,000
village laborers	240,600	272,836	288,579	326,441	357,158
agriculture[a]			240,010	259,111	278,890
industry[a]			7980	9304	
construction			10,236	12,458	
transportation			3068	4101	
commerce			3006	3947	
other			24,279	37,520	
social services[b]				1043	
education[c]				1445	
staff and workers	31,400	34,000	53,200	36,200	37,300
state		26,800[d]		22,000	22,500
urban collective		7200[d]		6000	5700
urban self-employed	470	765	955	1075	
Labor Force (2)			335,400		
primary industries[e]			242,500		
secondary[e]			76,400		
tertiary[e]			16,500		

a. "New" definitions (i.e., team and village enterprises included in appropriate sectors, rather than in agriculture).

b. Includes health care.

c. Includes cultural and broadcasting industries.

Table 4.2, continued

d. Obtained by applying 1984 shares to 1985 total: 1984 and 1985 totals differ by only 800.

e. Components of Gross Domestic Product.

Sources. Table A1, and: for 1985, Minnan85, pp. 244-45; for 1987: YHJJKF, pp. 420, 436-37; for 1990: FJNCTJ91, pp. 299, 301; FJTJNJ91, pp. 461, 463; for 1992: FJTJNJ93, pp. 439, 459.

  Agriculture. The share of the crop branch in Anxi's GVIAO *decreased* quite markedly during the 1980s (Figure 4.1). Looking within Anxi's agricultural sector alone, however, reveals that the share of crops in GVAO actually *increased*.[11] This seems contrary to the widely publicized goal of developing forest-based activities and the reported development of fisheries. On the other hand, Chapter 3 demonstrated that Anxi has also tried to modernize the crop and livestock branches and to restore production of local specialties. Tables 4.3 and 4.4 take a closer look at the effects of policy in these areas.

  Anxi's sown area and, in particular, the area sown to grain fell steadily in the early 1980s. The grain area reached a low of 638,100 mu in 1986 (14 percent below the 1980 level), as restructuring accelerated and, indeed, ran out of control. The provincial and county governments responded with tighter regulation of land use and with incentive programs designed to encourage grain production, and grain area partially recovered. In 1992, it was about 6 percent below the level of 1980. Improved farming techniques and increased use of modern inputs more than offset the decline; total output (though not output per capita) was higher in the early 1990s than in 1980. The area sown to all crops fully recovered, and then exceeded, the level of 1980, so that grain occupied a substantially smaller share of the total in the early 1990s as compared to a decade earlier.

  Among the major grain crops, the most conspicuous change is the introduction of corn and white potatoes. (See Tables A6 and A7.) In the early 1980s, these two crops accounted for no more than 1200 mu of sown area; by 1990, they accounted for over 56,400 mu—almost 8 percent of the total grain area. Conversely, the shares of rice in total area and total output declined slightly.

  Among crops other than grains, the 1980s saw pronounced movements into tea and into fruits, especially oranges, longan, and litchi (Table 4.3).[12] Tea area increased by almost 50 percent between 1980 and 1990; fruit area quadrupled between 1984 and 1990. By 1990, teas and fruits accounted for some 28.8 percent of the gross value originating in the crop branch, as compared to grain's 53.8 percent in the same year.[13] The

Table 4.3. Structure of Crop Production, 1980-92

	1980	1985	1987	1989	1990	1992
Sown Area (1000 mu)	817.3	769.1	801.7	837.3	864.7	852.4
grain	744.2	657.2	645.6	691.6	716.7	702.7
rice	$\approx 549^a$	506.4	468.0	504.7	504.7	
sweet potatoes		118.7	117.7	121.1	121.6	
other		32.1	59.9	65.8	90.4	
economic crops		43.4	36.3	32.9	33.7	30.1
peanuts	< 14	15.0		11.8	11.0	
sugar cane		15.8	9.3	7.5	8.6	
other		12.6		13.6	14.1	
other crops		68.6		112.8	114.3	119.6
Tea Area (1000 mu)	97	113.1	124.5^b	139.3	142.3	
Fruit Area (1000 mu)		33.3	44.7^b	92.5	112.4	

a. Estimated from data in Tables A6 and A7, by assuming that the growth rate of rice yield was the same as that of grain yield between 1980 and 1983.

b. 1986.

Source. Table A6.

growth of these crops has been driven by the promise of high incomes, partly attributable to preferential policies for fruit growers—and by the fact that they do not compete with grain for land.

Despite the increase in total sown area, there has been some movement out of cash (or "economic") crops, possibly reflecting the grain-enhancement efforts noted in Chapter 3. There may also have been some diversification *within* the cash-crop group—specifically, a shift out of sugar cane and peanuts, which accounted for 58 percent of cash-crop area in 1990, as compared to 67 percent in 1985. Vegetable area (included in the "other" subbranch, rather than in "economic" crops) increased markedly after 1985. As of 1990, "economic" crops accounted for only 5.8 percent

Table 4.4. Livestock, Forestry, and Fisheries, 1980-92

	1980	1985	1987	1989	1990	1992
Livestock (1000, year-end)						
cattle		53.5		57.8	59.1	
pigs	193.3	243.3	250.8	271.1	285.2	304.4[a]
sheep and goats		10.5		7.6	8.1	
poultry		1107		1624.4	1756	
Afforestation (1000 mu)		336.1		303.0	122.8	91.9
Fishponds (mu)		4151	4470[b]	4560	4560	
Output						
meat (tons)		11,566	12,401	13,864	14,448	16,093
dairy products (tons)		6		9	8	
eggs (tons)		327	479	528	564	592[a]
tung oil (tons)		41		16	19	
tea oil (tons)		288		134	97	
pine rosin (tons)		110		173	184	
timber (m^3)[c]		12,900		12,200	11,400	
bamboo (1000 stalks)[d]		777.6		520	410	
edible fungi (tons)			1026[e]	1732	f	f
fish (tons)	15	185	328	340	351	406

a. 1991.

b. 1986.

c. Village felling of timber.

d. Village cutting of bamboo.

e. 1988; for 1987: output value, 6.445 million yuan.

f. Increase on previous year.

Sources. For 1980: Minnan85, pp. 218-19. For 1985, 1989, and 1990: FJNCTJ91, pp. 169-92, except fungi, Huang, p. 255, and FJJJNJ91, p. 455. For 1987: Minnan87, p. 183; FJJJNJ87, p. 634; FJJJNJ88, pp. 724, 726; Huang, p. 255. For 1992: FJTJNJ93, p. 456; FJJJNJ93, p. 458; Minnan92, p. 204.

Table 4.5. Major Industrial Products and Exports, 1984-90

	Output			
	1984	1986	1989	Exports
Iron and iron ore (1000 tons)		432[a]		
Coal (1000 tons)	62.0	61.9	69.1	
Electric power (1000 kwh)	87.22	100.99	128	
Cement (1000 tons)	93	95.8		
Ammonium bicarbonate (tons)	23,494[b]	3048[c]		
Phosphate fertilizers (tons)	138[b]	222[c]		
Calcium carbide (tons)	1513	1382		
Plywood (square meters)	400	789		
Paper (tons)	1199	1358		
Lumber (cubic meters)	7500	6359		
Turpentine (tons)		31		
Sugar (tons)	2401	6414		
Processed tea (tons)	2138	4378		2452 (1984)
Edible oils (tons)		70		
Porcelain		193.3[d]		36.5[e] (1984)
Handicrafts (1000 USD)				396.9 (1984)
Textiles and apparel (1000 yuan)				3626 (1987)
Garments (1000 yuan)				84,640 (1990)
Tea processing equipment (units)	891	1247		
Other industrial equipment (units)				25 (1989)

a. Shipped from Pantian, 1985.

b. Actual weight.

c. Nutrient content.

d. 1000 pieces.

e. 1000 USD.

Sources: Zhang and Lu, pp. 576-77; FJJJNJ87, pp. 634-35; FJJJNJ88, p. 517; FJJJNJ90, p. 465; Huang, 258; FJRB, 20 September 1991, p. 2.

of the gross value originating in the crop branch, as compared to 8.4 percent for vegetables and (as noted earlier) 53.8 percent for grain.[14]

Table 4.4 collects data concerning non-crop branches of agriculture. The livestock branch remains heavily focused upon farmyard production of poultry and pigs; both industries have grown rapidly since the early 1980s. By contrast, efforts to develop the cattle, sheep, and dairy industries do not appear to have met with great success. Output of fish jumped sharply between 1983 and 1985, and continued growing through 1992, as the result of fishery projects initiated in the early 1980s. Interestingly, despite the *shan-hai* and two-front strategies noted in Chapter 3, production of several major forest products has fallen; it is not clear whether this reflects unprofitability during the later 1980s, imposition of controls over destructive exploitation of forests, or an effective effort to emphasize reforestation over current output.

Because developing and popularizing improved methods of growing grain and of raising pigs and poultry remained an important part of Anxi's development effort, these branches of agriculture have fared better in Anxi than elsewhere in eastern Fujian. Overall, the internal restructuring of agriculture in Anxi has been less pronounced than official policy might lead one to suspect—and certainly less pronounced than in many other counties. The most conspicuous change, and the one with the most pervasive implications for growth and welfare, is the growth of tea and fruit production on land unsuitable for field crops.

Industry. As shown in Figure 4.1 above, light industry grew somewhat more rapidly than heavy industry between 1978 and 1992—at roughly 19 percent per annum (in terms of GVIO in 1980 constant prices), as compared to 16 percent—both from very low bases.

Details on the structure of Anxi's GVIO by branch of industry have not been published for recent years. In 1984, the food-products industry was by far the county's most important, accounting for 51.7 percent of GVIO; chemicals, building materials, and electric power accounted for an additional 25 percent.[15] As shown in Table 4.5, during the mid 1980s, many of the county's principal industrial products and exports originated in these four industries and in mining. Subsequent reports indicate that the major industries of the mid 1980s experienced rapid growth during the late 1980s as well.[16] Of course, the data in Table 4.5 do not reflect the full impact of foreign-invested firms, mainly in the garment industry and other light industries, because this impact has been felt only in more recent years.

Table 4.6, in conjunction with Table 3.6, describes the structure of Anxi's industrial sector in the early 1990s, in terms of numbers of

Table 4.6. Industrial Enterprises, by Branch and Ownership, 1992

Branch	Ownership		
	state	collective	All
Mining: coal	2		2
Mining: ferrous metals		5	5
Mining and quarrying: non-metals		2	2
Lumber and bamboo	1		1
Water supply	1		1
Food products	10	8	18
Beverages			
alcoholic	2		2
tea	5	23	28
Feed	1		1
Textiles		1	1
Apparel		3	3
Leather products	1		1
Wood and bamboo products		4	4
Furniture	1	1	2
Paper	2	3	5
Printing	1	3	4
Cultural and athletic goods		2	2
Arts and crafts		4	4
Electric power, steam, and heated water	8	18	26
Chemicals	3	2	5
Pharmaceuticals	1		1
Rubber products		1	1
Plastics		2	2
Manufactures of non-metallic minerals	5	6	11

Table 4.6, continued

Branch	Ownership		
	state	collective	All
Ferrous metallurgy	1	1	2
Metal products	1	9	10
Machine building	3	11	14
Transport equipment	2	1	3
Electrical equipment		1	1
All	51	111	162

Note: At or above township level; not necessarily independent accounting units. Does not include foreign-invested enterprises (Table 3.6, above). No enterprises are listed in nine branches: mining of nonferrous metals; salt; tobacco products; coke, coal gas, and coal products; chemical fibers; nonferrous metallurgy; electronics and communications equipment; measuring devices and instruments; other.

Source. Table A9.

enterprises—but not, unfortunately, in terms of shares in output and employment. Table 4.6 classifies 162 state-owned and collective enterprises into 37 branches.[17] Beverages and food products account for 28 percent of the total, followed by electric power, machine building (mainly farm machines and tea-processing equipment), metal products (farm tools), products of non-metallic minerals (cement, bricks, and ceramics), mining and quarrying (coal, iron, manganese, and stone), and then chemicals and papermaking. Comparison of Table 4.6 with Table 3.6 suggests that the state and collective sectors have remained concentrated in accustomed branches, while the foreign-invested sector has brought new branches, such as garments and plastics, into the county.

Table 4.6 also shows that, of the 162 enterprises listed, almost one-third are state-owned—and that state ownership is not concentrated in any particular branch of industry. As shown in Table 4.7, when both foreign-invested enterprises and village-level enterprises are taken into account, the share of the state in GVIO was about 25 percent as of the early 1990s. Consistent with the development policy outlined in Chapter 3, the state's share had decreased sharply during the 1980s. By contrast, the share of industrial output originating in the smallest enterprises ("village and below," meaning enterprises operated by villages, partnerships, and individuals)

Table 4.7. Structure of Industrial Output, 1983-91

	1983	1984	1985	1986	1987	1988	1989	1990	1991
GVIO	48.0[a]	54.83[a]	95.11	93.49	136.92	195.44	224.19	276.52	317.69
state		44.69[a]			43.9	48.72	49.98	70.70	81.1
collective		10.09[a]			26.4				
other		0.05[a]			66.6				
GVIO		70.77	95.11	93.49	136.92	195.44	224.19	276.52	317.69
township and above			72.78	67.47	103.57[b]	141.49[c]	161.87	209.30	239.83
village and below	17.95[d]		22.32	26.02	31.76	53.77	62.26	67.01	77.63
urban, private[e]					1.59	0.18	0.06	0.21	0.23
GVIO, industrial enterprises only[f]					98.69	134.62	155.07	198.04	225.25
state					39.79		44.81	61.99	90.90
collective					21.86		35.06	41.48	48.11
other					37.04		75.20	94.57	86.53
GVIO, foreign-invested enterprises				14.06	33.04	64.03[g]	75.22[g]	90.79[g]	

Note: All values in million 1980 yuan. "New" definitions (i.e., team and village enterprises included in appropriate sectors rather than in agriculture), unless otherwise noted.

Table 4.7, continued

a. "Old" definitions: team (village) enterprises not included.

b. Of which: collective, 23.96 million.

c. Of which: collective, 28.80 million.

d. Team (village) enterprises only.

e. Coverage inconsistent; apparently included in "township and above" prior to 1987.

f. Industrial enterprises with independent accounts; see Table 4.8.

g. Pricing basis unspecified; probably 1980 constant prices.

Sources. For 1983-84: Minnan85, pp. 183, 212; Fujian shehui kexue yuan, p. 248; Zhang and Lu, p. 585. For 1985-86: Minnan86, p. 139; FJJJNJ87, p. 349. For 1987: YHJJKF, pp. 424-25; FJJJNJ89, p. 537; FJGYTJ88, pp. 308-09, 353, 361, 369. For 1988: FJJJNJ89, pp. 537-38; FJTJNJ89, pp. 504-05. For 1989: FJGYTJ90, pp. 192, 204, 209; FJJJNJ91, p. 455; FJJJNJ90, p. 465. For 1990: FJGYTJ91, 282-83; FJTJNJ91, p. 487; FJJJNJ91, p. 455. For 1991: FJGYTJ92, pp. 264-67; FJJJNJ92, p. 441; FJTJNJ92, p. 499.

increased to about one-fourth, and that of foreign-invested enterprises to almost one-third. The increasing weight of "village and below," and of FIEs like Anxing (which produces in dozens of rural workshops) suggest the possibility that industry is becoming more widely scattered across the county; as late as 1985, two-thirds of Anxi's GVIO had originated in the county's five towns, and only about one-third in the seventeen townships.[18]

Tables 4.8 through 4.10 compare the state, collective, and "other" sectors of industry, in terms of various indicators of enterprise size and productivity.[19] The data in the tables pertain to enterprises with independent accounts, rather than to all enterprises engaged in industry (e.g., to only 29 state-owned enterprises, rather than to the 51 noted in Table 4.6). Tables 4.8 through 4.10 reveal that, on average, state industrial enterprises are substantially larger than non-state enterprises in terms of employment and output, and are equipped with much larger stocks of plant and equipment (both absolutely and per worker). Reflecting the higher capital/labor ratio in state firms, they exhibit higher labor productivity—but lower capital productivity—than do non-state firms.

As suggested in Chapter 3, job creation is an important means of diffusing the benefits of growth. The state-owned enterprises in Table 4.8 accounted for about 5700 jobs in 1987 and 6400 jobs in 1991, at a cost of 121 million yuan in fixed assets by 1991; enterprises in the "other" category (Table 4.10) accounted for more jobs in both years at a fraction of the cost in terms of fixed assets (20 million yuan). As shown in the tables, the GVIO originating in "other" enterprises nearly equalled that of the state firms. Again, the data reflect the impact of enterprises such as Anxing,

Table 4.8. State Industrial Enterprises with Independent Accounts, 1987-91

	1987	1989	1991
number of enterprises	29	29	29
employment	5677	6356	6393
fixed assets (million yuan)			
original value	66.18	88.12	120.86
net value	50.29	67.63	90.39
GVIO (million 1980 yuan)	39.79	44.81	90.62[a]
profit and taxes (million yuan)[b]	8.74	11.99	16.33
employees per enterprise[c]	196	219	220
fixed assets per enterprise[c] (million yuan)			
original value	2.28	3.04	4.17
net value	1.73	2.33	3.12
fixed assets per employee (yuan)			
original value	11,658	13,864	18,905
net value	8859	10,640	14,139
GVIO per employee (1980 yuan)	7009	7049	14,175
GVIO per yuan of net fixed assets (1980 yuan)	0.79	0.66	1.00

Note: All values in current prices, unless otherwise indicated. Industrial enterprises with independent accounts satisfy three conditions: they have their own administrative structures, maintain their own accounts and take responsibility for profits and losses, and have the authority to enter contracts with other units and to set up bank accounts in their own name. A portion of industrial output originates in other enterprises (e.g., those operated as subsidiaries of schools, farms, etc.) that do not maintain independent accounts.

a. 1991 data converted from 1990 constant prices, using county deflator.

b. Sum of sales taxes and profit; this sum (routinely reported in provincial accounts) is distributed among various taxes, retained profit, and remitted profit.

c. Mean.

Sources. FJGYTJ88, pp. 346-72; FJGYTJ90, pp. 200-15; FJGYTJ91, p. 286; FJGYTJ92, pp. 264-85.

Table 4.9. **Collective Industrial Enterprises with Independent Accounts, 1987-91**

	1987	1989	1991
number of enterprises	107	97	98
employment	6022	10,302	4681
fixed assets (million yuan)			
original value	21.69	35.34	40.35
net value	15.62	25.35	26.47
GVIO (million 1980 yuan)	21.86	35.06	48.11[a]
profit and taxes (million yuan)[b]	5.72	6.58	8.16
employees per enterprise[c]	56	106	48
fixed assets per enterprise[c] (million yuan)			
original value	0.20	0.36	0.41
net value	0.15	0.26	0.27
fixed assets per employee (yuan)			
original value	3602	3430	8620
net value	2594	2461	5655
GVIO per employee (1980 yuan)	3630	3403	10,277
GVIO per yuan of net fixed assets (1980 yuan)	1.40	1.38	1.82

Notes and Sources: See Table 4.8.

which use large numbers of workers and simple techniques to produce consumer goods of relatively high value (as compared to factories in "smokestack" industries, which constitute a significant part of the state sector).

Tables 4.8 through 4.10 suggest that collective firms were hardest hit by the retrenchment of the late 1980s (or perhaps by more fundamental trends associated with reform and reopening). While both the state and "other" groups increased employment between 1987 and 1991, the collective group dismissed employees—and saw nine enterprises disappear.[20] Despite

Table 4.10. Other Industrial Enterprises with Independent Accounts, 1987-91

	1987	1989	1991
number of enterprises	5	13	24
employment	6733	9444	9224
fixed assets (million yuan)			
original value	3.51	10.94	20.02
net value	2.73	8.50	15.15
GVIO (million 1980 yuan)	37.04	75.20	86.53[a]
profit and taxes (million yuan)[b]	8.64	2.65	5.53
employees per enterprise[c]	1347	726	384
fixed assets per enterprise[c] (million yuan)			
original value	0.70	0.84	0.83
net value	0.55	0.65	0.63
fixed assets per employee (yuan)			
original value	521	1158	2170
net value	405	900	1642
GVIO per employee (1980 yuan)	5501	7963	9380
GVIO per yuan of net fixed assets (1980 yuan)	13.57	8.85	5.71

Note: "Other" includes all forms of ownership other than state and collective. For additional notes and for sources, see Table 4.8.

the decrease in employment, the collective group increased its stock of fixed assets, and maintained its share of GVIO.

In short, the available bits of evidence concerning the structure of Anxi's industrial sector reveal a shift toward light industry, toward non-state and market-oriented firms, and toward enterprises of smaller size and greater labor intensity. They also suggest, in the increasing weight of village-and-below firms, a shift toward more primitive technologies and a more dispersed geographical pattern of production.

B. Welfare

The ultimate objective of Anxi's development effort and of the structural changes pursued during the 1980s was, again, improvement in the welfare of Anxi residents. This section tries to draw some conclusions about welfare from (1) countywide output per capita, (2) countywide income, consumption, and savings per capita, and (3) bits of evidence concerning poverty alleviation.

Output per Capita. After fluctuating around a flat trend over the course of the Maoist era, real GVIAO per capita in Anxi grew at about 9.6 percent per annum between 1978 and 1992.[21] While certainly much better off now than in the late 1970s, Anxi remains poor: as of the early 1990s, the county's real GVIAO per capita had not yet reached the levels attained by Fujian's richer counties some fifteen years earlier, even before the start of reform and reopening. And Anxi is just beginning to see structural change on the scale experienced a decade ago in some such counties.[22]

Figure 4.3 looks more closely at the growth of GVIAO per capita in Anxi, relative to Jinjiang prefecture and Fujian province. Despite very rapid growth over more than a decade, Anxi has failed to keep pace with either the prefecture or the province. The relative gap between Anxi and Jinjiang prefecture increased from about 1:1.6 in 1978 and 1980 to 1:3.3 in 1992. As shown in the figure, the absolute gap widened markedly over the same period, approaching 1500 yuan by 1991. Hence, Anxi, while becoming better off in absolute terms, has also become poorer by comparison with its neighbors.

As noted earlier, NMP is a better indicator of aggregate output than is GVIAO. Anxi's real NMP per capita grew at about 6.2 percent per annum between 1983 (the first year for which NMP is reported) and 1992.[23] Again, the relative and absolute gaps between Anxi and Fujian and between Anxi and Jinjiang widened almost continuously, with an especially poor performance in 1989.[24] It is unclear why the economic downturn in that year—the first full year of retrenchment, and the year of Tiananmen—affected Anxi more seriously than the rest of the province and the rest of Jinjiang prefecture. Perhaps Anxi, having just begun to rely upon foreign investment as a source of growth, remained more susceptible to downturns in investor confidence than did areas where foreign-invested firms were more solidly established.

The growth performance of Anxi county is somewhat more impressive when measured against those of other designated poverty counties, rather than against that of the entire province or prefecture. The poverty

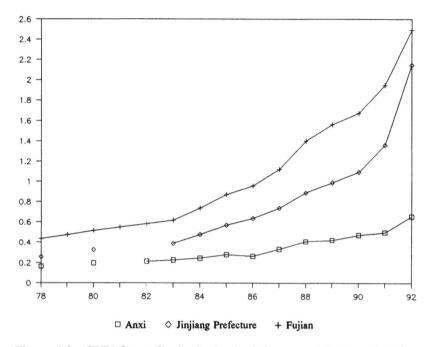

□ Anxi ◇ Jinjiang Prefecture + Fujian

Figure 4.3. GVIAO per Capita in Anxi, Jinjiang, and Fujian, 1978-92

Note. In thousands of 1980 constant yuan.

Sources. For Anxi and Fujian: Figure 1.1, above. For Jinjiang prefecture: Minnan85, pp 180, 183, 187; FJJJNJ86, pp. 624, 626; FJTJNJ86, pp. 41, 58; FJTJNJ87, pp. 28, 57; FJJJNJ88, pp. 33, 718; FJTJNJ89, pp. 503, 506; FJTJNJ90, pp. 451, 562; FJTJNJ92, pp. 473, 481; FJTJNJ93, pp. 437, 445.

counties share similar initial conditions, and were targeted with similar anti-poverty policies. Although Anxi remained the poorest of the seventeen poverty counties in terms of GVIAO and NMP per capita, it did grow slightly more rapidly than the group as a whole.[25]

Income, Consumption, and Savings. Conceptually, rural net income per capita is the best available indicator of household welfare in Anxi; rural net income includes income from all sources (in cash and kind), less production costs.[26] According to published reports, Anxi's rural net income per capita grew at an average annual rate of about 15 percent between 1983 and 1992, in nominal terms—or about 5.0 percent per annum, deflated by the provincial retail price index.[27] Even after several years of rapid growth, the rural net income per capita reported for 1990 was roughly

Table 4.11. Income and Consumption of Rural Households, 1984-90

	1984	1987	1989	1990
Net Income per Capita	220	357	482	546
Consumption per Capita	191	306.7	418.2	507.3
consumer goods	186	290.2	388.4	460.2
food			258.7	297.9
clothing			21.2	24.9
fuel			33.1	32.2
housing			31.9	52.5
other			43.5	52.6
other consumption[a]	5	16.4	29.8	47.1

Note: All data in current yuan.

a. E.g., services, entertainment.

Sources. FJTJNJ84, p. 229; FJTJNJ88, p. 556; FJNCTJ91, pp. 276-82.

the market value of 600 kilograms of rice—barely adequate to support the most spartan lifestyle. Unsurprisingly, income is allocated mainly to necessities—some 54 percent to food alone (Table 4.11). Saving is a small share of current income; however, by 1991 accumulated savings deposits amounted to 468 yuan per capita, about nine months' income.[28]

Figure 4.4 shows that the reported relative gaps between Anxi and Fujian province and between Anxi and Jinjiang prefecture narrowed somewhat between 1983 and 1992 in terms of rural net *income* per capita, despite the county's less impressive *output* performance. The relative income gap between Anxi and Fujian, for example, fell from 1:1.68 in 1983 to 1:1.40 in 1992 (both in nominal terms). The divergence between the output and income performances is partly attributable to remittances—and probably also reflects a large measure of error in the Anxi income data. (The time path shown in Figure 4.4 suggests that the reported incomes for Anxi are very rough estimates.)

Retail sales per capita in Anxi increased considerably during 1978-91 (Figure 4.5), although remaining low by comparison to the rest of Fujian. The increase in retail activity mirrors the increase in rural incomes (and in non-agricultural wages), and also a trend toward commercialization—from

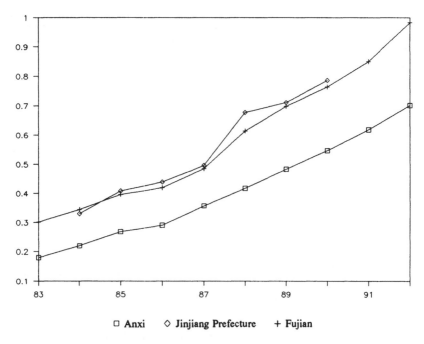

Figure 4.4. Rural Net Income per Capita in Anxi, Jinjiang, and Fujian, 1983-92

Note. In thousands of current yuan.

Sources. For Anxi: 1983, NMSR, p. 347. For Anxi and Jinjiang: 1984, FJJJNJ86, p. 628; 1985-86, FJJJNJ87, p. 920; 1987, FJJJNJ88, p. 733; 1988, FJTJNJ89, p. 525; 1989, FJTJNJ90, p. 511; 1990, FJTJNJ91, p. 504; 1991, FJTJNJ92, p. 513; 1992, FJTJNJ93, p. 477. For Fujian: FJTJNJ93, p. 160.

consumption of goods produced on farm to consumption of goods purchased in the marketplace. Rapidly increasing purchases from the agricultural sector (i.e., farmers' sales of their produce), noted in Chapter 3, also reflect this increasing commercialization.

The data reviewed so far do not capture the "social" components of welfare in Anxi—that is, the components not reflected in reported household incomes and expenditures. As noted in Chapter 2, during the Maoist era residents of Anxi enjoyed better access to education and, in particular, to health care than residents of other places with similarly low reported incomes. Abandonment of the commune regime may have caused some temporary disruption in delivery of "social" consumption goods; however, evidence surveyed in Chapter 3 (concerning construction of new schools and

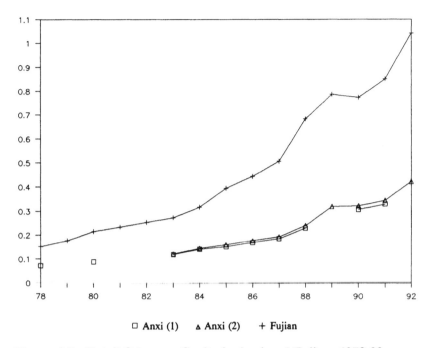

□ Anxi (1)   ▲ Anxi (2)   + Fujian

Figure 4.5. Retail Sales per Capita in Anxi and Fujian, 1978-92

Note. In thousands of current yuan. Fujian and Anxi (2) include sales by farmers directly to the non-agricultural population; Anxi (1) excludes such sales.

Sources. For Anxi (1): 1978-84, Minnan85, p. 227; 1985-86, FJJJNJ87, p. 635; 1987, Minnan87, p. 184; 1988, Minnan88, p. 169; 1990-91, Minnan92, p. 209. For Anxi (2): 1983-84, FJTJNJ84, p. 169; 1985-86, FJJJNJ87, p. 919; 1987, FJJJNJ88, p. 730; 1988, FJTJNJ89, p. 534; 1989, FJTJNJ90, p. 499; 1990, FJTJNJ91, p. 498; 1991, FJTJNJ92, p. 511; FJTJNJ93, p. 475. For Fujian: FJTJNJ93, pp. 44 and 314.

hospitals) clearly suggests that these goods were generally more accessible in the early 1990s than a decade earlier. County reports indicate that, as of 1992, fifteen towns and townships (up from nine in 1990) had implemented universal compulsory education at the elementary level, and two towns had implemented universal education through the lower-middle level. Countywide, the enrollment rate (in first grade) reportedly approached 100 percent.[29]

Poverty Alleviation. Countywide income per capita reveals little about the alleviation of poverty. Without additional information about the distribution of income, one cannot determine whether a few well-connected entrepreneurs and officials are capturing the bulk of the total increase in income, or whether it is benefitting a large number of needy households.

County reports, issued in connection with the anti-poverty campaign described in Chapter 3, do indicate that the increase in income in Anxi has been widely distributed. According to such reports, the number of households below the poverty line (200 yuan of 1985, per capita) fell from 58,482 in 1985 to 24,819 at the end of 1987, 6961 at the end of 1988, and 1170 by the end of 1990.[30] Income per capita in the ten designated poverty townships increased from 180 yuan in 1985 (67 percent of the countywide level) to 480 yuan in 1990 (88 percent) and 562 yuan in 1991 (91 percent).[31] County policy statements of the early 1990s claim that the poverty problem has been basically solved, and call for a shift from poverty relief to longer-term development efforts in poverty areas.[32]

While the 200-yuan standard is extremely low, virtually eliminating poverty over a period of five years—by even this standard—would stand as a notable achievement. Unfortunately, however, there is reason to doubt the veracity of poverty headcounts reported during the late 1980s. The performance of local cadres was measured, in part, by their success in reducing the number of households below the official poverty thresh-old—creating an incentive for undercounting of poor households as the anti-poverty campaign unfolded. In all likelihood, the truth is that many—but far from all—of the poverty-stricken have been made substantially better off. Foreign-invested firms created thousands of jobs for members of poverty-stricken households, and TVEs created thousands more. These injected into poor areas millions of yuan in wages, and created spillover benefits through local purchases of inputs and services. Poverty work teams introduced new marketable products (mushrooms, fruits, handicrafts) and, hence, new income streams, and provided thousands of poor people with rudimentary training in the necessary technical and business skills. Government and collective investment created temporary jobs in construc-tion (some subsidized by the national public-works program) and a permanent legacy of roads, telephone lines, potable water systems, power stations, and schools. And renewed access to relatives abroad brought in a flow of remittances and philanthropy that directly benefitted many of the poor.

Budgetary subsidies provided by the province have been important in maintaining income and, therefore, consumption and retail sales. The anti-poverty campaign, by transferring resources into the county, partially decoupled local incomes from local production; private remittances had a similar effect. Indeed, in Anxi rural net income per capita has routinely exceeded net material product per capita; this has occurred in only a few other counties.[33]   With respect to the stated goal of reducing local dependence upon provincial largesse (a goal noted in Chapter 3), then, Anxi cannot be said to have succeeded to any appreciable degree by the early 1990s.

C. Summary and Concluding Comments

As Anxi has veered away from the development path of the Maoist era, the county's economy has taken on a much more diversified structure, with substantial manufacturing and service sectors rising alongside a modernizing farm economy, and with new forms of private and hybrid enterprise overtaking state-run firms. Although no precise accounting is possible without household-level data, the benefits of growth appear to have been quite widely distributed, with a large share of the county's poverty-stricken households realizing increased private income as well as improved access to education and modern conveniences such as piped water and electric power.

Despite the attention to agriculture already noted, the evidence reviewed in this chapter clearly suggests that the main sources of Anxi's growth are to be found in industry. Foreign-invested firms, in particular, brought injections of capital and knowledge (both production technology and business acumen), thereby relieving the most important shortages constraining local development. Diffusion of technology and business skills, through subcontracting, emulation of FIEs, and hiring-away of FIE employees, multiplied the immediate impact of the FIEs themselves.

The data in Section A reflect the shifts in employment typically associated with early modern growth (i.e., shifts out of traditional activities of very low marginal productivity). In Anxi, workers have shifted out of grain production, into activities introduced through foreign-invested firms—and, more importantly, in terms of numbers of workers, through on-farm diversification and the emergence of small off-farm businesses. Such shifts are, of course, limited by the extent of the market—but the market accessible to Anxi has been expanding rapidly, as a result of market-oriented reform, increasing incomes across the Minnan region and the country, falling transport costs, and the marketing acumen supplied, in part, by overseas business partners.

Those employed in the grain and livestock branches—traditionally at the core of Anxi's economy—still constitute by far the largest group of workers in the county. Such workers are seeing their productivity increased by an improved ratio of farm labor to land (implicit in sectoral shift) and by yield increases (via introduction of new varieties and techniques and enhanced supplies of manufactured inputs).

Development assistance contributed significantly to Anxi's growth during the 1980s and to an accumulation of capital that will support future growth. National and provincial programs for poverty alleviation delivered budgetary subsidies to the county, placed other funds at the disposal of local governments, and provided consumer goods and technical assistance. As this development assistance tapers off, it is being partially replaced by the philanthropic activities of overseas Chinese, who now contribute substantial sums for schools, clinics, and other forms of social overhead capital. And construction of the Zhangping-Quanzhou railroad, undoubtedly a substantial boon to Anxi's development, represents a very substantial injection from outside the county.

Certain aspects of Anxi's post-Mao development path, such as continuing attention to the grain sector, are broadly reminiscent of the Maoist era. But an examination of the sources of growth since 1978—industry, private (and foreign) capital and knowhow, commercialization of agriculture, large investments in infrastructure—suggest that the nature of the development process is quite different.

Notes

1. The "sideline" branch of agriculture is excluded from GVIAO in Figure 4.1, due to inconsistencies in the "sideline" data over time. Because the sideline branch is small under the new accounting conventions adopted in the mid 1980s, this omission does not affect any of the major inferences to be drawn here.

2. See Figure 2.2, above. There is some inconsistency in definition between the two figures, due to the change in treatment of the sideline branch (note 1); correcting this inconsistency would not materially affect the comparison.

3. For 1985, ZGFXNC80-87, p. 205.

4. The average annual rate of increase is estimated from a trend line fitted to 11 annual observations. The comparison to rate of natural increase applies to 1980-88; FJRKTJ, pp. 180-196.

5. As noted in Chapter 3, the county has attempted to move surplus laborers into jobs in Quanzhou, Shishi and other cities of Jinjiang prefecture.

6. There appear to be two inconsistencies in the data underlying Table 4.2. First, the population residing outside Anxi's five towns shows a decline between 1986 and 1987, probably as a result of boundary changes in one or more of the towns. Second, the total population of Anxi jumps sharply in 1990, probably as a result of upward revision based on the 1990 census.

7. As of 1982, the median age in Anxi was 18.44 years, with only 3.26 percent of the population aged 65 or older, and 41.43 percent aged 14 or younger; FJRKTJ, p. 372.

8. Here, "agriculture" and "non-agricultural" pertain to employment rather than to household registration.

9. The "other" item is counted here as non-agricultural, since it includes mainly services (those that, in the SGV/NMP accounting system, are not included in the five "material-producing" sectors).

10. For GDP by sector in 1987, YHJJKF, p. 422. For GDP by sector in 1985 and 1991, see Table 4.1.

11. The share of crops in GVAO decreased sharply in Fujian as a whole and in many other counties; Fujian shehui kexue yuan, p. 200; FJTJNJ91, p. 478.

12. The area under tea and fruits is not included in sown area; however, production of teas and fruits is included in the crop branch of agriculture.

13. FJNCTJ91, pp. 47, 49; 1980 constant prices.

14. FJNCTJ91, p. 47; 1980 constant prices.

15. See Chapter 2, above.

16. E.g., FJJJNJ89, p. 537.

17. In 1986 Anxi had 175 state-owned and collectively owned industrial enterprises; FJJJNJ87, p. 634. The number of collective enterprises decreased somewhat in the late 1980s, as will be shown in Table 4.9 below. Hence, Table 4.6 appears to account for nearly all of the industrial enterprises in Anxi as of 1991-92.

18. Li, Chen, and Yu, pp. 386, 391, 397, 402, 407.

19. The single-factor productivity measures in the table are subject to a number of well-known deficiencies, the most important of which is the arbitrary nature of output and capital-stock valuation.

20. The retrenchment, initiated at the national level in late 1988, apparently hit with a lag of a year or more.

21. Calculated from a trend line fitted to 13 annual observations; see Figure 4.3, below.

22. For example, Anxi's GVIAO per capita in 1991 is comparable to that of Jiangle in 1978, and Anxi's 1991 GVIO per capita in 1991 is comparable to that of Jiangle in about 1983; Zhang and Lu, p. 323.

23. Calculated from a trend line fitted to 10 annual observations. The provincial NMP deflator is taken from FJTJNJ93, pp. 33, 35.

24. For Jinjiang: Minnan85, p. 182; FJJJNJ87, p. 912; FJJJNJ88, pp. 33, 717; FJTJNJ89, pp. 502-03; FJTJNJ90, p. 463; FJTJNJ91, p. 474; FJTJNJ92, p. 486; FJTJNJ93, p. 446. For Fujian: FJTJNJ93, pp. 33, 44.

25. Lyons 1992b.

26. As noted in Section A, some 94 percent of the population are agricultural; hence, the time path of rural household income reflects the welfare of the bulk of the county's population.

27. The price index is given in FJTJNJ93, p. 133.

28. FJJJNJ92, p. 441. Savings deposits per capita for all households are compared with the net income per capita of rural households (since rural savings cannot be isolated).

29. FJJJNJ91, p. 255; FJJJNJ93, p. 459. The enrollment rate, for 1987, was 96.80 percent; FJJJNJ88, p. 517.

30. FJJJNJ88, pp. 517-18; FJJJ, August 1988, p. 28; FJJJNJ89, p. 537; FJJJNJ91, p. 455; FJRB, 20 September 1991, p. 2.

31. FJRB, 20 September 1991, p. 2.

32. FJJJNJ91, p. 455; FJJJNJ92, p. 441.

33. Data for other counties are available in the sources cited in Figure 4.4 and note 23, above. In 1989, for example, income exceeded NMP in only four counties.

5
Conclusions

After many years with little improvement in output and income per capita, the Anxi economy reached a turning point in the late 1970s as Maoism was dismantled. Since then, the "South China miracle" has indeed reached into Anxi. While the changes it has worked there pale by comparison with those in Guangzhou or Xiamen, they are certainly welcome, and liberating, in a place so accustomed to deprivation.

The record leaves little doubt that the sources of Anxi's recent growth are intimately tied to changes in policy—and, specifically, to abandoning the autarkic stance characteristic of Maoism and accepting a greater degree of interdependence with other regions of China and with the rest of the world, admitting institutional changes conducive to greater interdependence and to individual initiative, and aggressively seeking after technical and business knowhow. Conversely, then, the stagnation of the Anxi economy prior to 1978 and the poverty of many thousands of households in the county were largely policy-induced. To some extent, investments undertaken prior to 1978 did pave the way for subsequent growth; still, an earlier tempering of the Maoist policy regime could have accelerated that growth and, in the process, alleviated a great deal of suffering. The people of Anxi were not well served by Maoism.

Anxi in Context. Perhaps Anxi is, among the counties of South China, an extreme example, in terms of the extent of poverty associated with Maoist prescriptions. But Anxi is hardly exceptional in the overall contours of its post-Mao experience; many other counties have grown more rapidly and realized larger improvements in welfare. Indeed, extrapolating from Anxi's experience, one might infer that the development of South China during the 1980s was in large part a process of catching up, by

117

undoing past errors and escaping the massive burdens they exacted in the form of forgone growth.

Looking a bit more closely at the specifics of Anxi's development path reveals many elements, such as the emergence of a new sector of private and hybrid enterprise and efforts to commercialize and restructure village economies, that are widely observed in other counties as well. On the other hand, central and provincial decisions have left considerable latitude for local differentiation, and local decision-makers have clearly taken advantage of this latitude. It may not be going too far to suggest that a distinctive "Anxi model" of development emerged, melding outward-oriented industrialization and village commercialization with continuing emphasis on grain and livestock. This model differs from those associated with Jianyang, Jinjiang, Dongshan, Gutian, and other Fujian counties whose development paths have merited comment in the provincial press.[1] Needless to say, the precise contours of the "Anxi model" cannot be replicated by counties lacking Anxi's dense overseas network—just as the Dongshan and Gutian models cannot be replicated by other counties lacking conditions so well suited to producing asparagus and mushrooms.

The emergence of such "models" is, of course, entirely consistent with the call for regional (and local) differentiation that has permeated central policy pronouncements during the 1980s and early 1990s. In fact, calls for adaptation of policy to suit local conditions were commonplace during the Maoist era. It is only over the past decade or so, however, that a measure of genuine adaptation and differentiation are evident, in the experiences of Anxi and other locales.

Then again, the instruments deployed in implementing policy are in some ways unchanged. The attack on poverty in Anxi, for example, is a classic instance of the mobilization campaign, so familiar in China under Mao; the attack on poverty has been replete with the slogans, the precise—though arbitrary—targets, and the work teams characteristic of campaigns. Many policy pronouncements show the familiar proclivity toward general prescriptions that are pleasing to the ear—though they are of questionable substance: every village should specialize in one commodity (why not two or three?), every household should plant fruit trees (why not pine or bamboo?).

Prospects. Despite the rapid growth and the improvements in welfare realized since the late 1970s, Anxi remains poor. A substantial share of the rural households in the county are, at best, hovering a bit above bare subsistence, with little in the way of real property or human capital. The sorts of projects that have served to generate modest, if very important, increases in the incomes of such households—fruit trees, mushrooms, geese, bamboo-working—are unlikely to propel all of them into the modern world. In some cases, termination of the public assistance now propping up incomes will plunge families back into poverty. Many other families remain susceptible to backsliding, with the loss of a crop or the collapse of a sideline venture.

On the one hand, being backward in a prosperous, commercialized region might augur well for Anxi's continued growth: perhaps Anxi can reasonably expect to be dragged along by the booming regional economy around it. As coastal cities and towns develop, benefits will spill down in greater volume to Anxi and other relatively distant places. With the emergence of labor shortages along the coast and the widening of wage differentials, more firms may come into Anxi in search of cheap labor. FIEs firmly established in Xiamen or Quanzhou may begin to look farther afield for cheap building sites and for local governments still willing to offer generous concessions so as to attract industry—and still blind to the new forms of environmental damage now blighting much of the region. And, in any case, the rapid growth of consumption in booming coastal cities will increase demand for Anxi's products.

On the other hand, progress is increasingly linked to competitiveness. Anxi now competes not only for the political favor that yields railroad projects or "preferential" policies, but also in the markets for various exports and for inbound FDI; these are forms of competition that the county did not face a decade ago. Insofar as industry is concerned, Anxi could easily remain little more than a pool of unskilled labor, competitive only so long as the labor in other areas of Fujian, and in other countries, remains marginally more expensive. Substantial investments in human capital—in building and repairing schools, in universal elementary education, and in technical and business training—indicate that the county leadership recognizes this hazard, but provide no guarantee that local businesses will in fact compete successfully in more knowledge-intensive industries. And, of course, Anxi's openness, besides bringing rapid growth, has made the county vulnerable to new risks, even in agriculture. A collapse of the market for longan or mushrooms could cause rural incomes to plunge across much of the county.

Anxi's own long history of outmigration and the experiences of poor rural areas around the world point to the possibility that the county may simply empty out. Rather than a continuing influx of higher-paying jobs, Anxi could see the bulk of its young people move to cities and towns—Xiamen and Quanzhou, and now also Shishi and Jinjiang. Restrictions on relocation are certain to ease, and the rapid growth of local incomes during the post-Mao era may well have spawned an even more rapid spiralling of expectations.

Notes

1. Concerning the experiences of other counties, see Lyons 1992b. Briefly, the four models noted in the text emphasize, respectively, forest products and grain, labor-intensive manufactures, asparagus and fishing, and mushrooms (and trade in mushrooms).

Appendix

This appendix presents basic data used at various points throughout the book and summarized in many of the tables and figures already discussed. Five types of data are collected here, with full documentation as to sources:

(1) population (for 1949-92) with agricultural and non-agricultural components (for most years); labor force (for 1984-92 and, for benchmark years only, 1952-80) with village and other components;

(2) aggregate output—GVIAO with components (for 1982-92 inclusive and for numerous years during 1949-80); NMP (for 1978 and 1983-92) with sectoral components (for 1989-92); GNP and GDP (for 1978 and 1985-92) with GDP components (for most years since 1985);

(3) detailed agricultural data—total cultivated area, total sown area, and grain output (1949-92); areas sown to, and output of, various crops (1980-92);

(4) detailed industrial data—identification and description of state-owned, collective, and foreign-invested enterprises as of the early 1990s;

(5) data concerning the economies of Anxi's five towns, c1985-89.

Table A1. Population and Labor Force, 1949-92

Year	Population (year-end)			Labor Force			
	total	agricul- tural	non- agricul- tural	total	village	staff[a]	urban self- employed
1949	299,370						
1950	309,463	301,463	8000				
1951	319,898						
1952	330,434	317,934	12,500	154,600	152,600	2000	
1953	348,092						
1954	358,875						
1955	367,285						
1956	380,052	361,604	18,448				
1957	390,300	368,500	21,800	154,400	149,100	5300	
1958	394,380	368,511	25,869				
1959	400,239	366,367	33,872				
1960	408,080	367,412	40,668				
1961	409,445	387,591	21,854				
1962	427,186	410,340	16,846	166,000	159,900	6100	
1963	443,361	421,515	21,846				
1964	454,837	436,659	18,178				
1965	470,272	450,872	19,400	174,100	166,500	7600	
1966	490,934	471,604	19,330				
1967	509,226	483,306	25,920				
1968	530,879	503,953	26,926				
1969	548,999	533,677	15,322				
1970	562,423	548,375	14,048	213,600	202,600	11,000	
1971	578,948	564,804	14,144				
1972	601,860	582,746	19,114				
1973	621,042	600,954	20,088				

Table A1, continued

	Population (year-end)			Labor Force			
Year	total	agricul-tural	non-agricul-tural	total	village	staff[a]	urban self-employed
1974	636,049	611,759	24,290				
1975	652,962	627,509	25,453				
1976	673,219	647,081	26,138	239,800	224,700	15,100	
1977	691,802	665,261	26,541				
1978	706,690	679,233	27,457	250,500	230,900	26,700	
1979	718,462	688,028	30,434				
1980	728,628	696,562	32,066	272,000	240,000	31,400	470
1981	742,654	707,755	34,899				
1982	760,349	724,232	36,117				
1983	770,746	733,796	36,950				
1984	782,685	744,499	38,186	296,700	262,900	33,200	586
1985	792,766	748,102	44,664	310,400	272,836	34,000	765
1986	802,667	757,281	45,386	315,200	277,100	38,000	2235
1987	814,141	766,757	47,384	342,700	288,579	53,200	955
1988	826,883	778,269	48,600	346,000	300,000	45,800	1029
1989	846,485	796,863	49,622		313,230	31,300	
1990	916,204	865,104	51,100	363,716	326,441	36,200	1075
1991	928,400	877,000	51,400	378,960	340,331	37,900	729
1992	943,900	891,300	52,600		357,158	37,300	

a. Staff and workers in state units and urban collectives.

Sources. For population, 1949-88: FJRKTJ; Zhang and Lu, pp. 584-85; FJJJNJ87, p. 635. For population, 1989-92: FJJJNJ90, p. 25; FJJJNJ91, p. 33; FJTJNJ92, p. 473; FJTJNJ93, p. 437. For labor force, Zhang and Lu, pp. 584-85; FJJJNJ87, p. 635; Minnan85, p. 249; Minnan86, pp. 138, 140; Minnan 87, p. 185; Minnan88, pp. 158, 179; Minnan92, p. 212; FJTJNJ88, p. 517; FJTJNJ89, p. 538; FJTJNJ90, p. 452; FJTJNJ91, p. 463; FJTJNJ92, p. 475, 495; FJTJNJ93, pp. 439, 459; FJNCTJ91, p. 299.

Table A2. Gross Value of Industrial and Agricultural Output, 1949-92

Year	GVIAO	on old definitions[a]		on new definitions[b]	
		GVAO	GVIO	GVAO	GVIO
1949	30,130	29,060	1070		
1950	33,020	31,730	1290		
1952	41,350	39,240	2110		
1957	62,050	53,840	8210		
1962	41,330	32,830	8500		
1965	62,650	52,590	9700		
1966	67,900	56,000	11,900		
1969	60,020	45,750	14,270		
1970	69,660	54,220	15,440		
1976	87,170	63,420	23,750		
1978	113,410	80,310	33,100	73,730	39,690
1980	141,850	98,450	43,500	79,650	50,520
1982	158,100				
1983	171,910	123,910	48,000	105,960[c]	65,960[c]
1984	188,990	134,160	54,830	118,220	70,770
1985	219,780	144,950	74,830	124,760	95,110
1986	209,520			116,030	93,490
1987	268,880			129,240	136,920
1988	334,480			139,040	195,440
1989	352,580			128,390[d]	224,190
1990	414,690			138,170	276,520
1991	464,300[e]			146,610[e]	317,690[e]
1992	612,960[e]			149,350[e]	463,610[e]

Note: Thousands of 1980 constant yuan throughout.

a. Team and village sidelines included in agriculture.

Table A2, continued

b. Team and village sidelines included in industry.

c. Estimated by moving reported output of village and team sidelines from agriculture (on old definitions) to industry.

d. Decrease from 1988 may be due to changes in coverage; see Huang, p. 255.

e. Converted from 1990 prices, using county-level sectoral deflators.

Sources. For 1949-85 (old definitions): Zhang and Lu, pp. 573, 584-85; FJJJNJ87, pp. 634-35; FJTJNJ83, pp. 44, 83; Minnan85, pp. 183, 207; FJTJNJ84, p. 92; FJTJNJ86, p. 42; Population Census Office, p. 175. For 1978-85 (new definitions): Zhang and Lu, p. 585; FJJJNJ87, p. 634; Fujian shehui kexue yuan, p. 200; Minnan85, p. 212; Minnan86, p. 137. For 1986-92: FJJJNJ87, p 635; FJTJNJ88, p. 33; FJTJNJ89, p. 506; FJTJNJ90, p. 462-63; FJTJNJ91, p. 478, 487; FJTJNJ92, p. 490, 499; FJTJNJ93, p. 454, 463.

Table A3. Net Material Product, 1978-92

Year	Total	Agriculture	Industry	Construc-tion	Transport-ation	Commerce
1978	74,600					
1983	132,340					
1984	155,460					
1985	189,290					
1986	196,280					
1987	240,060					
1988	320,880					
1989	326,150	158,780	96,800	21,320	12,120	37,130
1990	378,480	194,000	106,000	27,000	10,000	41,000
1991	441,000	217,000	137,000	38,000	13,000	36,000
1992	576,000	247,000	198,000	70,000	17,000	44,000

Note: Thousands of current yuan throughout.

Sources. Minnan85, p. 182; FJJJNJ86, p. 622; FJJJNJ87, p. 911; FJJJNJ88, pp. 538, 717; FJTJNJ89, p. 503; FJTJNJ90, p. 459; FJTJNJ91, p. 471; FJTJNJ92, p. 482; FJTJNJ93, p. 446.

Table A4. GNP and GDP, 1978-92

Year	GNP	GDP	Primary	Secondary	Tertiary
1978	93,080				
1985		210,410	108,360	59,970	42,080
1986	247,520				
1987	301,750	278,800	112,640	94,730	71,430
1988	393,260				
1989	408,050	383,640	158,120	117,520	108,000
1990	477,000	454,000	194,000	135,000	126,000
1991	560,000	544,000	217,000	174,000	153,000
1992	724,000	701,000	246,000	265,000	190,000

Note: Gross National Product and Gross Domestic Product originating in Anxi; thousands of current yuan throughout.

Sources. Fujian shehui kexue yuan, p 22; YHJJFK, p. 422; FJJJNJ88, pp. 516-17; FJJJNJ89, p. 538; FJTJNJ89, p. 506; FJJJNJ90, p. 456; FJJJNJ91, p. 465; FJTJNJ92, p. 477; FJTJNJ93, p. 441.

Table A5. Crop Area and Output, 1949-79

				Grain Output (tons)	
Year	Cultivated Area	Total Area Sown	Area Sown to Grain	old series	new series
1949	430,860	609,457	577,121	65,180	56,050
1950	430,870	617,093	584,765	71,711	
1951	433,190	621,887	588,209	77,957	
1952	435,940	628,794	592,104	85,875	81,546
1953	427,500	641,294	587,337	86,801	
1954	426,370	663,011	606,584	94,143	
1955	430,100	706,954	632,116	107,335	
1956	462,610	924,303	863,048	127,051	
1957	475,410	929,191	870,912	127,721	118,608
1958	430,010	922,633	838,641	140,850	
1962					83,730
1965					119,921
1966					a
1967					a
1968					a
1969					a
1975		898,146	798,284		146,052
1976		877,065	786,142		127,819
1977		855,032	770,400		151,240
1978		853,700	790,100		158,048
1979		849,249	723,335		147,882

Note: For 1980-92, see Tables A6 and A7.

a. Below pre-1966 peak.

Sources. For areas and old grain series: provincial annual reports. For new grain series: Zhang and Lu, pp. 574; FJJJNJ87, pp. 634-35.

Table A6. Cultivated and Sown Area, 1980-92

	1980	1982	1983	1984	1985	1986
Cultivated Area (1000 mu)	411.3		410	407.7	405.3	403.2
Sown Area (1000 mu)	817.3	807	797.5	780.9	769.1	770.1
grain	744.2	722	719.2	688.4	657.2	638.1
rice			543	528.1	506.4	500
wheat			42	31.1	23.9	15
sweet potatoes			≈125	120.8	118.7	116
white potatoes						
corn				0		0
soy	7.0[a]	7.3	8	7.5	7.1	6
economic crops		36	28.5	39.1	43.4	39
oil crops	14		14	13.3	15.0	13
peanuts				12.0	13.3	
rapeseed					0.8	
bast fibers				0.5	0.5	<0.1
sugar cane			6	12.4	15.8	14
tobacco			4	5.1		4
flue-cured					1.3	
other crops		49	49.8		68.6	
vegetables					58.9	
green manures			7	4.1	2.7	2
Tea Area (1000 mu)	97			104	113.1	124.5
Fruit Area (1000 mu)				27	33.3	44.7
oranges					7.5	
longan, litchi					4.6	
bananas					3.2	

Table A6, continued

	1987	1988	1989	1990	1991	1992
Cultivated Area (1000 mu)	400.6	399.0	398.1	395.7	394.5	393.0
Sown Area (1000 mu)	801.7	815	837.3	864.7	855.3	852.4
grain	645.6	655	691.6	716.7	702.3	702.7
rice	468.0		504.7	504.7		
wheat	21.8		20.3	24.1		
sweet potatoes	117.7		121.1	121.6		
white potatoes	0		36.7	43.3		
corn	1.9		0.6	13.1		
soy	5.8		6.3	6.1		
economic crops	36.3		32.9	33.7	33.8	30.1
oil crops	13.9	13		11.0		
peanuts			11.8	11.0		
rapeseed			0.3	0.1		
bast fibers	0					
sugar cane	9.3		7.5	8.6		
tobacco	4.1					
flue-cured			0.1	0.4		
other crops			112.8	114.3	119.2	119.6
vegetables			106.1	107.7		
green manures	1.9		5.0	5.2		
Tea Area (1000 mu)			139.3	142.3		
Fruit Area (1000 mu)			92.5	112.4		
oranges			21.7	23.9		
longan, litchi			15.8	20.7		
bananas			2.5	2.1		

Note: No 1981 data are available. Sources follow Table A7; see p. 132.

a. 1979.

Table A7. Output of Field Crops, Tea, and Fruits, 1980-92

	1980	1982	1983	1984	1985	1986
Field Crops (1000 tons)						
grain	166.9	162.2	176.3	154.2	147.9	128.8
rice	135.2		146.1	127.0	122.1	107.7
wheat			1.9	2.6	2.1	1.6
sweet potatoes	26.7		≈27.9	24.1	23.3	19.1
white potatoes						
corn				0		0
soy	0.2[a]		0.4	0.4	0.4	0.4
economic crops						
oil crops	1.2		1.5	1.4	1.6	1.5
peanuts		≈1.6		1.4	1.5	1.5
rapeseed			0.1		<0.1	
bast fibers			0.1	0.1	0.1	0.1
sugar cane			26.4	56.7	70.6	49.7
tobacco			0.3	0.3		0.3
flue-cured			0.1		0.1	
other crops						
vegetables						
Tea (1000 tons)				3.0	4.0	4.1
Fruit (1000 tons)		≈1.8		2.2	2.8	3.7
oranges					0.6	
longan, litchi					0.6	
bananas					0.7	

Table A7, continued

	1987	1988	1989	1990	1991	1992
Field Crops (1000 tons)						
grain	145.3	148.2	163.6	167.2	169.4	178.7
rice	120.2		133.7	134.4		
wheat	2.2		2.8	2.9		
sweet potatoes	22.2		22.2	22.5		
white potatoes	0		4.3	5.7		
corn	0.2		0.1	0.1		
soy	0.4		0.4	0.4		
economic crops						
oil crops	1.6	1.5	1.4	1.3	1.0	1.2
peanuts			1.4	1.3		
rapeseed			<0.1	<0.1		
bast fibers						
sugar cane	40.6	34.5	30.6	33.6	39.6	32.2
tobacco	0.3	0.3	0.2			
flue-cured			<0.1	<0.1		
other crops						
vegetables	76.2		b	b		
Tea (1000 tons)	5.2	5.9	6.4	7.0	9.0	7.5
Fruit (1000 tons)	4.9	5.0	4.5	4.4	5.6	5.4
oranges			1.5	1.6		
longan, litchi			0.9	0.7		
bananas			0.7	0.6		

Note: No 1981 data are available.

a. 1979.

b. Increase over previous year.

132

Table A6, continued

Sources. For 1980 and 1982: ZGFX80-87, p. 205; Fujian sheng cehui ju, following p. 36; provincial annual reports. For 1983, 1984, 1986, and 1987: unpublished data collected by Bruce Stone, International Food Policy Research Institute, except 1983 other crop area from provincial annual report, 1984 tea and fruit from Zhang and Lu, p. 574, and Minnan85, p. 122, 1986 tea and fruit from FJJJNJ87, p. 634. For 1985, 1989, 1990: FJNCTJ91, pp. 94-164. For 1988: ZGFX88, pp. 82-83. For 1991 and 1992: FJTJNJ92, pp. 492, 494; FJJJNJ92, pp. 604-08; FJTJNJ93, p. 458.

Table A7, continued

Sources. For 1980 and 1982: ZGFX80-87, p. 205; Fujian sheng cehui ju, following p. 36; Minnan85, p. 217; Chen Jilin, pp. 154, 163; provincial annual reports. For 1983, 1984, 1986, and 1987: unpublished data collected by Bruce Stone, International Food Policy Research Institute, except 1983 flue-cured tobacco from FJTJNJ83, p. 56, 1984 tea and fruit from Zhang and Lu, p. 574, and Minnan85, p. 122, 1986 tea and fruit from FJJJNJ87, p. 634, 1987 oil crops and vegetables from YHJJKF, pp. 434-35, and 1987 tea and fruit from FJJJNJ88, p. 724. For 1985, 1989, 1990: FJNCTJ91, pp. 94-164, except vegetables, FJJJNJ90, p. 465, and FJJJNJ91, p. 455. For 1988: ZGFX88, pp. 82-83; FJJJNJ89, pp. 781-82. For 1991 and 1992: FJTJNJ92, pp. 492; FJTJNJ93, p. 456.

Table A8. Foreign-Invested Enterprises, 1991

	Enterprise	Type[a]	Registered Capital (1000 USD)[b]	Year Approved	Office Address	Comments
1	Anxing Rattanware	jv	486	1984	Fengcheng	furniture and housewares; ranked 88th in exports in Fujian in 1991
2	Fenghua Clothing	jv	500, initial; 1,210, as of 1992	1985	Fengcheng	athletic apparel; ranked 24th in exports in Fujian, 1991
3	Qingshuiyan Investment[c]	cv	167	1985		operational as of July 1985
4	Wanan Chemical[c]	cv	137	1985		shampoo; operational as of January 1986
5	Yuanyuan Sundries[c]	jv	205			umbrellas; operational as of March 1987
6	Chengjin Foods	jv	134	1987	Fengcheng	preserved foods; operational as of October 1987
7	Xingan Sundries[c]	jv	270		Penglai	umbrellas, garments; operational as of June 1988
8	Huahuang Clothing	jv	270	1988	Fengcheng	raingear, garments; operational as of November 1988
9	Hongtai Clothing	jv	270	1988	Fengcheng	raingear, garments; operational as of November 1988
10	Jinfeng Maternitywear	jv	140	1988	Fengcheng	garments
11	Anda Magnetic Tape	jv	210	1988	Hutou	blank video tapes

Table A8, continued

	Enterprise	Type[a]	Registered Capital (1000 USD)[b]	Year Approved	Office Address	Comments
12	Lianda Clothing	jv	400	1989	Fengcheng	garments; raingear
13	Fengkui Clothing	jv	270	1989	Kuidou	
14	Anxing Garment	jv	418	1989	Fengcheng	offshoot of Anxing Rattanware
15	Yuxing Garment Knitting	jv	190	1989	Fengcheng	
16	Hongsheng Clothing	jv	160	1989	Fengcheng	
17	Xinan Magnetic Tape	jv	210	1989	Fengcheng	
18	Anxing Artificial Flower	jv	192	1989	Fengcheng	offshoot of Anxing Rattanware
19	Ganglian Woolens	wfo	250	1989	Fengcheng	knitted goods
20	Linyuan Raingear	wfo	256	1989	Fengcheng	
21	Jiantai Weaving	jv	287	1990	Fengcheng	belts, bags
22	Xincheng Garment	jv	127	1990	Fengcheng	
23	Huafa Clothing	jv	340	1990	Fengcheng	
24	Lihong Handicrafts	jv	106	1990	Fengcheng	
25	Mingsheng Paint	jv	212	1990	Fengcheng	
26	Dongcheng Clock and Watch	jv	159	1990	Fengcheng	clock and watch components
27	Yuquan Tea	wfo	254	1990	Xiping	

Table A8, continued

	Enterprise	Type[a]	Registered Capital (1000 USD)[b]	Year Approved	Office Address	Comments
28	Mingxing Knitting	wfo	128	1990	Fengcheng	rubber products
29	Qingan Furniture	wfo	500	1990	Penglai	
30	Lisheng Rubber	wfo	161	1990	Chengxiang	
31	Fangzheng Sundries	wfo	256	1990	Jingu	
32	Wanan Auto Parts	wfo	190	1990	Fengcheng	
33	Mingli Garment	wfo	128	1990	Chengxiang	
34	Anxi Instant Tea	jv	677	1991	Shangqing	tea, coffee, and fruit juice
35	Xinxin Clothing	wfo	256	1991	Fengcheng	
36	Xingfeng Electronics	jv	564	1991	Fengcheng	salvage of scrapped components
37	Sandexing Development	wfo	714	1991	Fengcheng	development of industrial districts
38	Xinhua Clothing	jv			Fengcheng	

a. Jv: equity joint venture; cv: cooperative joint venture; wfo: wholly foreign owned.

b. Initial, unless otherwise indicated; when reported in yuan: converted at the official exchange rate. "Registered capital" is "the total investment reported to administrative authorities by all parties to the venture;" increases in capital must also be approved and registered. Reported contributions to registered capital determine the partners' shares in the enterprise. The foreign investors must contribute at least 25 percent in an equity joint venture.

c. May have ceased operation or merged by 1990.

Sources: Minnan88, pp. 108-09; FJWSTZ, pp. 166-98; Minnan92, pp. 100-36; FJRB, 2 October 1990, p. 2; FJRB, 17 February 1991, p. 2; FJRB, 13 June 1991, p. 3; FJRB, 28 July 1991, p. 4; FJRB, 8 January 1992, p. 8; ZGGYQY; for detail on registered capital, Yang and Lou, p. 510.

Table A9. State- and Collectively-Owned Industrial Enterprises, 1992

	Enterprise	Ownership	Location[a]	Comments
1	Anxi Coal Mine	state	Jiandou	
2	Fuqian Farm Coalpit	state	Fuqian state farm	
3	Pantian Iron Mine	collective	Gande	reorganized in 1988
4	Taozhou Township Mining Company	collective	Taozhou[b]	iron mining
5	Jingu Manganese Mine	collective	Jingu	
6	Shangqing Mining Development Company	collective	Shangqing	manganese mining
7	Shangqing Township Ore-Dressing Plant	collective	Shangqing	
8	Tiefeng Stone Company	collective	Guanqiao	flagstone, other stone products, handicrafts
9	Longmen Resource Development Company	collective	Longmen	stone slabs
10	Anxi Lumber Company	state	Fengcheng	
11	Anxi Waterworks	state	Fengcheng	
12	Chengguan Grain Processing Plant	state	Fengcheng	rice, flour
13	Hutou Grain Processing Plant	state	Hutou	rice, feed
14	Guanqiao Grain Processing Plant	state	Guanqiao	rice, rice noodles
15	Xiping Grain Processing Plant	state	Xiping	rice, flour products, feed
16	Longjuan Grain Processing Plant	state	Longjuan	rice, flour products
17	Changkeng Grain Processing Plant	state	Changkeng	rice, flour products

Table A9, continued

	Enterprise	Ownership	Location[a]	Comments
18	Gande Grain Processing Plant	state	Gande	rice, flour products, feed
19	Fuqian Grain Processing Plant	state	Fuqian State Farm	
20	Anxi Food Products Plant	state	Fengcheng	preserved foods, candied fruits, cakes
21	Hutou SMC[c] Confectionery	collective	Hutou	candy, cakes
22	Longmen SMC[c] Confectionery	collective	Longmen	candy, cakes
23	Penglai SMC[c] Confectionery	collective	Penglai	candy, cakes
24	Penglai Food Products Plant	collective	Penglai	candy
25	Guanqiao Food Products Plant	collective	Guanqiao	candy, cakes
26	Xiping Food Products Plant	collective	Xiping	confections
27	Longjuan Food Products Plant	collective	Longjuan	biscuits, grain processing, wine
28	Anxi Sugar Mill	state	Fengcheng	medium-sized
29	Fengcheng Neighborhood[d] Food Products Plant	collective	Fengcheng	
30	Anxi Distillery	state	Fengcheng	liquor; ethyl alcohol
31	Fuqian Distillery	state	Fuqian State Farm	rice wine
32	Anxi Tea Plant	state	Guanqiao	established 1952; 1991: ranked 55th in exports in Fujian, at 37.34 million yuan
33	Huqiu SMC[c] Tea Plant	collective	Huqiu	

Table A9, continued

	Enterprise	Ownership	Location[a]	Comments
34	Xiping SMC[c] Tea Plant	collective	Xiping	
35	Shangqing SMC[c] Tea Plant	collective	Shangqing	
36	Guanqiao SMC[c] Tea Plant	collective	Guanqiao	
37	Jiandou SMC[c] Tea Plant	collective	Jiandou	
38	Longjuan SMC[c] Tea Plant	collective	Longjuan	
39	Lantian SMC[c] Tea Plant	collective	Lantian	
40	Huqiu Vocational School Tea Plant	collective	Huqiu	
41	Fuqian Tea Plant	state	Fuqian State Farm	
42	Tongmei Tea Plant	state	Tongmei State Farm	
43	Lutian Tea Farm Tea Plant	state	Lutian	
44	Anxi County Tea Import/Export Company Tea Plant	state	Fengcheng	
45	Anxi Scented Wulong Tea Plant	collective	Penglai	
46	Guanqiao Tea Company	collective	Guanqiao	
47	Jiandou Tea Company	collective	Jiandou	
48	Jingu Tea Processing Plant	collective	Jingu	
49	Jingu Tea and Fruit Processing Plant	collective	Jingu	
50	Huqiu Township Tea Company	collective	Huqiu	

Table A9, continued

	Enterprise	Ownership	Location[a]	Comments
51	Daping Tea Company	collective	Daping	
52	Xiping Tea Processing Company	collective	Xiping	one of Fujian's largest TVEs; 1988 GVIO: 17 million yuan
53	Lutian Township Tea Company	collective	Lutian	
54	Lantian Township Tea Processing Company	collective	Lantian	
55	Lantian Tea Farm Tea Processing Plant	collective	Lantian	established 1988; 1991 GVO: 1.5 million yuan
56	Lantian Tea Plant	collective	Lantian	
57	Xianghua Tea Processing Company	collective	Xianghua	
58	Gande Township Tea Plant	collective	Gande	
59	Shangqing Township Tea Processing Company	collective	Shangqing	
60	Anxi Grain Bureau Feed Mill	state	Fengcheng	
61	Anxi Down Factory	collective	Fengcheng	down products
62	Xinxin Garment Factory	collective	Fengcheng	
63	Kuidou Shoe and Garment Factory	collective	Kuidou	shoes, gloves
64	Jingu Clothing Factory	collective	Jingu	
65	Anxi Leather Factory	state	Fengcheng	
66	Anxi Plywood Factory	collective	Fengcheng	
67	Taozhou Wood Products Factory	collective	Taozhou[b]	

Table A9, continued

	Enterprise	Ownership	Location[a]	Comments
68	Fengtian Wood and Bamboo Products Factory	collective	Fengtian	
69	Fengcheng Neighborhood[d] General Factory	collective	Fengcheng	bamboo and rattan products
70	Anxi Wooden Furniture Factory	collective	Fengcheng	
71	Anxi County General Factory	state	Fengcheng	wooden furniture
72	Anxi County Paper Mill	state	Gande	
73	Jin-An Paper Mill	collective	Chengxiang	
74	Anxi Printed Carton Factory	state	Chengxiang	
75	Kuidou Packing Materials Factory	collective	Kuidou	
76	Jinqiao Cement Sack Factory	collective	Jingu	
77	Anxi Printing	state	Fengcheng	
78	Yizhong Printing	collective	Fengcheng	
79	Fengcheng Printing	collective	Fengcheng	
80	Jingu Printing	collective	Jingu	
81	Anxi Wuzhong Educational Materials Factory	collective	Xiping	established 1975; abacuses
82	Fengcheng Chemical Plant	collective	Fengcheng	colored paper, chalk, paste
83	Anxi Bamboo Products Factory	collective	Fengcheng	woven bamboo products
84	Jingu Bamboo and Rattan Plant	collective	Jingu	
85	Anxi County Foreign Trade Company Drawnwork Factory	collective	Fengcheng	

Table A9, continued

	Enterprise	Ownership	Location[a]	Comments
86	Changkeng Fireworks Factory	collective	Changkeng	
87	Xianrong Power Plant	state	Jiandou	prefectural; thermal; built 1971
88	Fuqian Power Plant	state	Fuqian State Farm	hydro
89	Anxi County Lutian Power Plant	state	Lutian	hydro
90	Anxi County Penglai Sanyingdao Power Plant	state	Penglai	hydro
91	Anxi County Huoshaoqiao Reservoir Hydroelectric Station	state	Hutou	
92	Anxi County Cunnei Reservoir Power Plant	state	Longmen	hydro
93	Banlin Tree Farm Power Plant	state	Banlin State Farm	hydro
94	Penglai Power Plant	collective	Penglai	hydro
95	Hutou Power Plant	collective	Hutou	hydro
96	Guanqiao Power Plant	collective	Guanqiao	hydro
97	Jiandou Chaobi Power Plant	collective	Jiandou	hydro; opened 1986; 1.2 megawatts
98	Cannei Power Plant	collective	Cannei	hydro
99	Kuidou Township Power Plant	collective	Kuidou	hydro
100	Jingu Power Plant	collective	Jingu	hydro
101	Bailai Power Plant	collective	Bailai	hydro
102	Shangqing Power Plant	collective	Shangqing	hydro

Table A9, continued

	Enterprise	Ownership	Location[a]	Comments
103	Longmen Township Power Plant	collective	Longmen	hydro
104	Huqiu Power Plant	collective	Huqiu	hydro
105	Xiping Power Plant	collective	Xiping	hydro
106	Longjuan Power Plant	collective	Longjuan	hydro
107	Changkeng Power Plant	collective	Changkeng	hydro
108	Xianghua Power Plant	collective	Xianghua	hydro
109	Gande Power plant	collective	Gande	hydro
110	Anxi County Power Company	state	Fengcheng	established 1985; urban electric service
111	Huqiu Power Buerau	collective	Huqiu	electric service
112	Gande Power Company	collective	Gande	electric service
113	Anxi County Electrometallurgy Plant	state	Hutou	
114	Anxi County Chemical Fertilizer Factory	state	Jiandou	
115	Anxi County Pine Rosin Factory	state	Xiping	
116	Anxi Mosquito Repellant Factory	collective	Chengxiang	
117	Shangqing Public Welfare Factory	collective	Shangqing	paints
118	Anxi Pharmaceuticals Factory	state	Fengcheng	
119	Anxi Tire Recapping Plant	collective	Chengxiang	
120	Anxi Plastics Factory	collective	Fengcheng	plastic film; plastic bags

Table A9, continued

	Enterprise	Ownership	Location[a]	Comments
121	Jiandou Plastic Foam Plant	collective	Jiandou	sponges
122	Anxi County Cement Plant	state	Jiandou	established 1963; capacity, 1991: 76,000 tons
123	Hutou Cement Plant	state	Hutou	
124	Jiandou Cement Plant	collective	Jiandou	
125	Gande Cement Plant	collective	Gande	established 1976; 1991 GVO: 1.45 million yuan
126	Fuqian Brick and Tile Plant	state	Fuqian State Farm	
127	Chengxiang Brick and Tile Plant	collective	Chengxiang	
128	Kuidou Building Materials Processing Plant	collective	Kuidou	ceramics
129	Anxi County Porcelain Factory	state	Kuidou	
130	Longmen Porcelain Factory	collective	Longmen	
131	Anxi County Fire-Retardant Materials Factory	state	Hutou	fire-resistant bricks and cement
132	Shangqing Graphite Plant	collective	Shangqing	established 1970; 1991 GVO: 5 million yuan
133	Anxi County Iron and Steel Plant	state	Jiandou	
134	San-An Ferro-Alloy Company	collective	Gande	venture with Sanming Steel
135	Anxi Metal Crafts Factory	collective	Fengcheng	metal products for household use
136	Penglai Hardware Factory	collective	Penglai	

Table A9, continued

	Enterprise	Ownership	Location[a]	Comments
137	Anxi Iron-Working Factory	collective	Changkeng	small agricultural implements; tea-processing equipment
138	Jiandou Agricultural Machinery Plant	collective	Jiandou	small agricultural implements
139	Kuidou Agricultural Machinery Plant	collective	Kuidou	small agricultural implements
140	Jingu Agricultural Machinery Plant	collective	Jingu	small agricultural implements
141	Shangqing Agricultural Machinery Plant	collective	Shangqing	small agricultural implements
142	Xianghua Agricultural Machinery Plant	collective	Xianghua	small agricultural implements
143	Tongmei Farm Electroplating Plant	state	Tongmei State Farm	
144	Longgang Metal Products Plant	collective	Longmen	
145	Huqiuma Steel Plant	collective	Huqiu	established 1977; auto parts, castings
146	Anxi County Chemical Industry Equipment Factory	state	Jiandou	established 1971; parts
147	Nanqiao Machinery Company	collective	Fengcheng	industrial machinery
148	Shangqing Township Machine Parts Factory	collective	Shangqing	parts for industrial machinery
149	Anxi County Tea Machinery Factory	state	Fengcheng	established 1950s; equipment for processing Wulong tea
150	Penglai Agricultural Machinery Factory	collective	Penglai	

Table A9, continued

	Enterprise	Ownership	Location[a]	Comments
151	Longmen Agricultural Machinery Factory	collective	Longmen	castings for farm machines
152	Huqiu Agricultural Machinery Factory	collective	Huqiu	tea equipment
153	Xiping Agricultural Machinery Factory	collective	Xiping	iron farm machines
154	Lutian Agricultural Machinery Factory	collective	Lutian	tea equipment
155	Longjuan Agricultural Machinery Factory	collective	Longjuan	threshers
156	Anxi Metal Products and Electrical Equipment Factory	collective	Fengcheng	bicycle parts
157	Fuqian Agricultural Machinery Plant	state	Fuqian State Farm	repairs
158	Anxi Light Machinery Factory	collective	Fengcheng	coal-washing equipment
159	Fujian Province #1 Construction Company Machinery Repair Depot	state	Fengcheng	repair of transport equipment
160	Anxi Auto Repair	state	Fengcheng	
161	Anxi Transport Repair and Parts	collective	Fengcheng	established 1979
162	Anxi Electrical Equipment Factory	collective	Hutou	transformers

Note: At or above township level; not necessarily independent accounting units. Does not include foreign-invested enterprises (listed in Table A8, above).

a. Town or township.

b. Taozhou Township was established in the late 1980s, from the northwestern part of Gande.

c. Supply and Marketing Cooperative.

d. *Jiedao*.

Sources: ZGGYQY; FJJNJ89, p. 120.

Table A10. Towns (*zhen*) in Anxi

	Fengcheng	Hutou	Penglai	Guanqiao	Jiandou
Land area (km²)	14.14	15.84	122	106.1	121.48
Total population, year-end					
1985	23,123	16,797	58,994	60,494	32,338
1986	23,923	16,665	59,484	61,368	32,320
1987	24,968	62,041	60,196	62,279	32,473
1988	25,777	62,533	61,625	63,177	32,667
1989	26,745	63,147	63,012	64,450	32,805
Non-agricultural population, year-end					
1985	12,840	5939	1367	2968	3560
1986	13,557	5747	1705	3064	3318
1987	14,404	7063	1823	3050	3278
1988	14,985	7024	1839	3315	3268
1989	15,416	7075	1879	3405	3282
Economic structure, 1985					
labor force	11,002	8938	23,694	25,658	10,826
agriculture	2770	4025	18,761	17,989	5475
industry	1783	1736	463	1526	3410
construction	1272	488	1335	2472	157
transport	440	585	265	385	988
commerce	2015	1024	1040	547	409
other	2722	1080	1830	2739	387

Table A10, continued

	Fengcheng	Hutou	Penglai	Guanqiao	Jiandou
GVIAO (mn. yuan)[a]	21.1	7.483	9.689	34.638	14.251
GVAO	1.64	1.476	7.669	8.654	3.664
GVIO	19.46	6.007	2.02	25.984	10.587
state	11.024	4.08	1.03	22.379	8.201
collective[b]	3.79	0.575		1.292	0.745
village and below	1.69	0.895	0.8	2.213	1.641
urban individual	0.8	0.457		0.1	
other	2.156	0		0	
industrial enterprises	66	17	18	7	15
state	18	8		1	8
collective	45	9	8	6	7
other	3			0	0
investment in fixed assets (mn. current yuan)	7.766	4.591	4.2	6.863	8
freight volume (th. tons)	120				1470
freight turnover (mn. ton-km)	14.54				
passenger volume (th. persons)	2400			540	223
passenger turnover (mn. person-km)	81.88			1.31	
commercial establishments	649	206	524	292	234
private sector[c]	575	118	501	290	185
retail sales (mn. yuan)	41.5	29.09	7.473	8.43	5.844

Table A10, continued

	Fengcheng	Hutou	Penglai	Guanqiao	Jiandou
trade in farmers' markets (mn. yuan)	5.7	5.383	2	3	1.097
urban residential space (th. m²)	228	63.2	11.3	41.1	35.5
major industrial products	processed tea	chemicals	auto parts	processed tea	processed tea
	machines	machines	canned foods	electric power	coal
	food products	electric power	tools	tiles	fertilizer
	wine	food products	processed tea	bricks	cement
	bambooware	cement		sand	electric power
	rattanware	calcium carbide		granite	lumber
	watches	fertilizer			
	shampoo	bricks			
	moldings	tiles			
	printed matter	transformers			
		plastics			
		tractor parts			

Note: The towns of Penglai, Guanqiao, and Jiandou are spatially equivalent to townships. The town of Hutou is located in Hutou township, but is administratively distinct from it. Similarly, the town of Fengcheng is located in Chengxiang township.

a. Price basis not specified; probably 1980 constant yuan.

b. Town/township level and above.

c. *Getihu*.

Source: Li, Chen, and Yu, pp. 382-407; FJJNJ87, p. 41; FJJNJ88, p. 40; FJJNJ89, p. 19; FJJNJ90, p. 35; FJJNJ93, p. 459.

References

CD. *China Daily*, various issues. Beijing.

Chen Gengzhong and Chen Zhehui. "Wai yin nei lian: Anxi jingji fazhan de genben chulu" [Absorb from abroad, and cooperate domestically: the fundamental path for Anxi's economic development]. In *Zou xiang 21 shiji: Fujian sheng gaige kaifang yu fazhan zhanlue [Toward the 21st Century: Reform, Opening Up and Development Strategy in Fujian]*, ed. Fujian sheng jiwei jingji yanjiu suo [Fujian Planning Commission, Economic Research Office], pp. 163-68. Beijing: Zhongguo wujia, 1992.

Chen Jiayuan. *Fujian jingji dili*. Beijing: Xinhua, 1991.

Chen Jilin. *Fujian jingji dili*. Fuzhou: Fujian kexue jishu, 1985.

Cheng, H. H. "Regional Development of Agriculture in China with Special Reference to Red Soil." In *Agricultural Reform and Development in China*, ed. T C. Tso, pp. 369-74. Beltsville, MD: Ideals, Inc., 1990.

Crook, Frederick W. "Underreporting of China's Cultivated Land Area: Implications for World Agricultural Trade." *China* (United States Department of Agriculture, Situation and Outlook Series, RS-93-4), July 1993, pp. 33-39.

Falkenheim, Victor Carl. "Provincial Administration in Fukien: 1949-1966." PhD dissertation, Columbia University, 1972.

FJFJ. Fujian sheng tongji ju [Fujian Statistical Bureau]. *Fujian fenjin de sishi nian [Forty Years of Progress in Fujian]*. Beijing: Zhongguo tongji, 1989.

FJGYTJ88. Fujian sheng tongji ju [Fujian Statistical Bureau]. *Fujian gongye tongji nianjian 1988 [Fujian Industrial Statistical Yearbook 1988]*. Beijing: Zhongguo tongji, 1988.

FJGYTJ90. Fujian sheng tongji ju. *Fujian gongye jingji tongji nianjian 1990*. Beijing: Zhongguo tongji, 1990.

FJGYTJ91. Fujian sheng tongji ju. *Fujian gongye jingji tongji nianjian 1991*. Beijing: Zhongguo tongji, 1991.

FJGYTJ92. Fujian sheng tongji ju. *Fujian gongye jingji tongji nianjian 1992*. Beijing: Zhongguo tongji, 1992.

FJJJ. *Fujian jingji [Fujian's Economy]*, various issues. Fuzhou; monthly.

FJJJNJ85. Fujian jingji nianjian bianji weiyuanhui [Fujian Economic Yearbook Editorial Board]. *Fujian jingji nianjian 1985 [Fujian Economic Yearbook 1985]*. Fuzhou: Fujian renmin, 1985.

FJJJNJ86. Fujian jingji nianjian bianji weiyuanhui. *Fujian jingji nianjian 1986*. Fuzhou: Fujian renmin, 1986.

FJJJNJ87. Fujian jingji nianjian bianji weiyuanhui. *Fujian jingji nianjian 1987*. Fuzhou: Fujian jingji nianjian bianjibu, 1987.

FJJJNJ88. Fujian jingji nianjian bianji weiyuanhui. *Fujian jingji nianjian 1988*. Fuzhou: Fujian jingji nianjian she, 1988.

FJJJNJ89. Fujian jingji nianjian bianji weiyuanhui. *Fujian jingji nianjian 1989*. Fuzhou: Fujian jingji nianjian she, 1989.

FJJJNJ90. Fujian jingji nianjian bianji weiyuanhui. *Fujian jingji nianjian 1990*. Fuzhou: Fujian renmin, 1990.

FJJJNJ91. Fujian jingji nianjian bianji weiyuanhui. *Fujian jingji nianjian 1991*. Fuzhou: Fujian renmin, 1991.

FJJJNJ92. Fujian jingji nianjian bianji weiyuanhui. *Fujian jingji nianjian 1992*. Fuzhou: Fujian renmin, 1992.

FJJJNJ93. Fujian jingji nianjian bianji weiyuanhui. *Fujian jingji nianjian 1993*. Fuzhou: Fujian renmin, 1993.

FJNCTJ91. Fujian sheng tongji ju, nongcun chu [Fujian Statistical Bureau, Rural Statistics Office]. *Fujian sheng nongcun tongji nianjian 1991 [Fujian Rural Statistical Yearbook 1991]*. Beijing: Zhongguo tongji, 1991.

FJNYDQ. Fujian sheng jihua weiyuanhui [Fujian Planning Commission]. *Fujian nongye daquan [Encyclopedia of Fujian Agriculture]*. Fuzhou: Fujian renmin, 1991.

FJNYKJ. *Fujian nongye keji [Fujian Agricultural Science and Technology]*, various issues. Fuzhou; bimonthly.

FJRB. *Fujian ribao [Fujian daily]*. various issues. Fuzhou.

FJRKTJ. Fujian sheng tongji ju [Fujian Statistical Bureau]. *Fujian sheng renkou tongji ziliao huibian 1949-1988 [Compilation of Statistical Materials on Fujian's Population, 1949-88]*. Beijing: Zhongguo tongji, 1989.

FJSHTJ. Fujian sheng tongji ju [Fujian Statistical Bureau]. *Fujian shehui tongji ziliao [Fujian Social Statistics]*. Fuzhou: Fujian sheng tongji ju, 1986.

FJSYTJ86-90. Fujian sheng tongji ju, maoyi chu [Fujian Statistical Bureau, Trade Office]. *Fujian shangye tongji nianjian 1986-1990 [Fujian Commerce Statistical Yearbook, 1986-90]*. Beijing: Zhongguo tongji, 1991.

FJTJNJ83. Fujian sheng tongji ju [Fujian Statistical Bureau]. *Fujian tongji nianjian 1983 [Fujian Statistical Yearbook 1983]*. Fuzhou: Fujian renmin, 1983.

FJTJNJ84. Fujian sheng tongji ju. *Fujian tongji nianjian 1984*. Fuzhou: Fujian renmin, 1985.

FJTJNJ86. Fujian sheng tongji ju. *Fujian tongji nianjian 1986.* Fuzhou: Fujian renmin, 1986.

FJTJNJ87. Fujian sheng tongji ju. *Fujian tongji nianjian 1987.* Beijing: Zhongguo tongji, 1987.

FJTJNJ88. Fujian sheng tongji ju. *Fujian tongji nianjian 1988.* Beijing: Zhongguo tongji, 1988.

FJTJNJ89. Fujian sheng tongji ju. *Fujian tongji nianjian 1989.* Beijing: Zhongguo tongji, 1989.

FJTJNJ90. Fujian sheng tongji ju. *Fujian tongji nianjian 1990.* Beijing: Zhongguo tongji, 1990.

FJTJNJ91. Fujian sheng tongji ju. *Fujian tongji nianjian 1991.* Beijing: Zhongguo tongji, 1991.

FJTJNJ92. Fujian sheng tongji ju. *Fujian tongji nianjian 1992.* Beijing: Zhongguo tongji, 1992.

FJTJNJ93. Fujian sheng tongji ju. *Fujian tongji nianjian 1993.* Beijing: Zhongguo tongji, 1993.

FJWSTZ. Fujian sheng tongji ju [Fujian Statistical Bureau]. *Fujian waishang touzi qiye daguan [Directory of Foreign-Invested Enterprises in Fujian].* Beijing: Zhongguo tongji, 1991.

Fujian shehui kexue yuan [Fujian Academy of Social Sciences]. *Minnan sanjiao kaifangqu fazhan zhanlue yanjiu [Research on Development Strategies for the Southern Fujian Open Area].* Shanghai: Shanghai shehui kexue yuan, 1989.

Fujian sheng cehui ju [Fujian Cartographic Bureau]. *Fujian sheng dituce [Fujian Atlas].* Fuzhou: Fujian ditu, 1982.

Fujian sheng jiaotong ting [Fujian Transport Bureau]. *Fujian jiaotong shouce [Fujian Transportation Handbook].* Fuzhou: Fujian kexue jishu, 1981.

Fujian sheng zhengfu [Government of Fujian]. *Fujian ziliao huibian (diyi ji) [Compilation of Materials on Fujian (no. 1)]*. Taipei: Fujian Government, 1957.

Fujian shifan daxue dili xi, Fujian ziran dili bianxiezu [Fujian Teachers' College, Geography Department, Editorial Board for Natural Geography of Fujian]. *Fujian ziran dili [Natural Geography of Fujian]*. Fuzhou: Fujian renmin, 1987.

Fuzhou shi guiguo huaqiao lianyihui [Fuzhou Society of Returned Overseas Chinese]. *Fujian guiqiao shouce [Handbook for Overseas Chinese Returning to Fujian]*. Fuzhou: Fuzhou shi guiguo huaqiao lianyihui, 1956.

Gardella, Robert P. "The Boom Years of the Fukien Tea Trade, 1842-1888." In *America's China Trade in Historical Perspective*, ed. Ernest R. May and John K. Fairbank, pp. 33-75. Cambridge: Harvard University Press, 1986.

Huang Zhenhua. "Liang wei zhu, lin wei ben, cha tuo pin, guo zhi fu" [Taking grain and forests as the foundation, develop tea to escape poverty and fruits to become rich]. In *Fujian yanhai kaifangqu jingji zonghe kaifa yanjiu* [Research on Overall Economic Development of the Fujian Open Area], ed. Zhonggong fujian shengwei zhengce yanjiu shi [Policy Research Office of the Fujian Communist Party Committee], pp. 254-66. Xiamen: Lujiang, 1991.

Johnson, Graham. "Open for Business, Open to the World: Consequences of Global Incorporation in Guangdong and the Pearl River Delta." In *The Economic Transformation of South China: Reform and Development in the Post-Mao Era*, ed. Thomas P. Lyons and Victor Nee, pp. 55-87. Ithaca: Cornell University, East Asia Program, 1994.

Lardy, Nicholas R. *Agriculture in China's Modern Economic Development*. Cambridge: Cambridge University Press, 1983.

Li Qixiang, Chen Jian, and Yu Ming. *Fujian xiao chengzhen [Fujian's Small Cities and Towns]*. Fuzhou: Fujian ditu, 1988.

Liang Heng. "Contractual Arrangements and Labor Incentives in Rural China in the 1980s." PhD dissertation, Cornell University, 1993.

Lin Jinzhi and Zhuang Weiji. *Jindai huaqiao touzi guonei qiye shi ziliao xuanji (fujian juan) [Materials Concerning Overseas Chinese Investment in Domestic Enterprises (Fujian)].* Fuzhou: Fujian renmin. 1985.

Lyons, Thomas P. *Economic Integration and Planning in Maoist China.* New York: Columbia University Press, 1987.

Lyons, Thomas P. "Grain in Fujian: Intraprovincial Patterns of Production and Trade." *China Quarterly*, no. 129 (March 1992a), pp. 184-215.

Lyons, Thomas P. *China's War on Poverty: A Case Study of Fujian Province, 1985-1990.* Hong Kong: Chinese University, 1992b.

Lyons, Thomas P. "Commercial Reform in China: The Grain Trade of Fujian Province, 1978-1988." *Economic Development and Cultural Change*, 41 (July 1993), pp. 691-736.

Minnan85. Xiamen shi tongji ju [Xiamen Municipal Statistical Bureau]. *Minnan sanjiao diqu ji Xia-Zhang-Quan jingji kaifangqu shehui jingji gaikuang [Social and Economic Overview of the Southeastern Fujian Region and the Xiamen-Zhangzhou-Quanzhou Economic Open Area].* Xiamen: Xiamen shi tongji ju, 1985.

Minnan86. Xiamen shi tongji ju. *Minnan sanjiao diqu 1986 nian shehui jingji gaikuang [Social and Economic Overview of the Southeastern Fujian Region in 1986].* Xiamen: Xiamen shi tongji ju, 1987.

Minnan87. Xiamen shi tongji ju. *Minnan sanjiao diqu 1987 nian shehui jingji gaikuang.* Xiamen: Xiamen shi tongji ju, 1988.

Minnan88. Xiamen shi tongji ju. *Minnan sanjiao diqu 1988 nian shehui jingji gaikuang.* Xiamen: Xiamen shi tongji ju, 1989.

Minnan92. Xiamen shi tongji ju. *Minnan sanjiao diqu 1992 nian shehui jingji gaikuang.* Xiamen: Xiamen shi tongji ju, 1992.

Nee, Victor. "A Theory of Market Transition." *American Sociological Review.* 54(5), October 1989, pp. 663-81.

Nee, Victor, and Su Sijin. "Institutional Change and Economic Growth in China: The View from the Villages." *Journal of Asian Studies,* 49(1), February 1990, pp. 3-25.

Nee, Victor, and Young, Frank. "Peasant Entrpreneurs in China's Emerging Market Economy: An Institutional Analysis." *Economic Development and Cultural Change,* 39, 1991, pp. 293-310.

Nickum, James E. "Volatile Waters: Is China's Irrigation in Decline?" In *Agricultural Reform and Development in China,* ed. T. C. Tso, pp. 284-96. Beltsville, MD: Ideals, Inc., 1990.

NMSR. Guojia tongji ju, nongcun chouyang diaocha zongdui [State Statistical Bureau, Rural Sample Survey Team]. *Gesheng zizhiqu zhixiashi nongmin shouru xiaofei diaocha yanjiu ziliao huibian [Collection of Research Materials from the Farmer Income and Consumption Survey, by Province, Autonomous Region, and Municipality].* Beijing: Zhongguo tongji, 1985.

Nolan, Peter. *Growth Processes and Distributional Change in a South China Province: The Case of Guangdong.* London: University of London, School of Oriental Studies, 1983.

Nongye bu renmin gongshe guanli ju [Ministry of Agriculture, Commune Management Bureau]. "1977-1979 quanguo qiong xian qingkuang" [Conditions in poor counties nationwide, 1977-79]. *Xinhua yuebao,* February, 1981, pp. 117-20.

Oi, Jean C. "The Fate of the Collective after the Commune." In *Chinese Society on the Eve of Tiananmen,* ed. Deborah Davis and Ezra Vogel, pp. 15-34. Cambridge: Harvard Council on East Asian Studies, 1990.

Population Census Office of the State Council, *The Population Atlas of China.* Hong Kong: Oxford University Press, 1987.

Prime, Penelope. "Industry's Response to Market Liberalization in China: Evidence from Jiangsu Province." *Economic Development and Cultural Change*, 41(1), 1992, pp. 27-50.

Putterman, Louis. "People's Republic of China: Systemic and Structural Change in a North China Township." *American Journal of Agricultural Economics*, 70, May 1988, pp. 423-30.

Putterman, Louis. "Entering the Post-Collective Era in North China: Dahe Township." *Modern China*, 15, 1989, pp. 275-320.

Reynolds, Bruce L. "Two Models of Agricultural Development: A Context for Current Chinese Policy." *China Quarterly*, no. 76 (December 1978), pp. 842-72.

Riskin, Carl. *China's Political Economy*. New York: Oxford University Press, 1987.

Rozelle, Scott D. "The Economic Behavior of Village Leaders in China's Reform Economy." PhD dissertation, Cornell University, 1991.

Stone, Bruce. "Basic Agricultural Technology under Reform." In *Economic Trends in Chinese Agriculture*, ed. Y. Y. Kueh and Robert F. Ash, pp. 311-60. New York: Oxford, 1993.

SYC81. State Statistical Bureau. *Statistical Yearbook of China 1981*. Beijing: Statistical Publishing House, 1982.

SYC85. State Statistical Bureau. *Statistical Yearbook of China 1985*. Hong Kong: Economic Information and Agency, 1985.

Vermeer, Eduard B. *Economic Development in Provincial China: The Central Shaanxi Since 1930*. Cambridge: Cambridge University Press, 1988.

Vermeer, Eduard B. "Land Reclamation in the Hills and along the Coast of Fujian: Recent History and Present Situation." In *Remaking Peasant China: Problems of Rural Development and Institutions at the Start of the 1990s*, ed. Jorgen Delman, Clemens Stubbe Ostergaard, and Flemming Christiansen, pp. 158-78. Aarhus: Aarhus University Press, 1990.

Vogel, Ezra. *One Step Ahead in China: Guangdong under Reform.* Cambridge, MA: Harvard University Press, 1989.

Weng Junyi. "Economic Growth in Fujian Province: A Growth-Center Analysis, 1950-91." In *The Economic Transformation of South China: Reform and Development in the Post-Mao Era*, ed. Thomas P. Lyons and Victor Nee, pp. 88-117. Ithaca: Cornell University, East Asia Program, 1994.

World Bank. *World Development Report 1984.* New York: Oxford University Press, 1984.

World Bank. *China: Growth and Development in Gansu Province.* Washington: World Bank, 1990.

World Bank. *World Development Report 1993.* New York: Oxford University Press, 1993.

Yang Jiwan and Lou Erxing. *Jingji da zidian (kuaiji juan) [Dictionary of Economics (Accounting)].* Shanghai: Shanghai cishu, 1991.

YHJJKF. Guojia tongji ju [State Statistical Bureau]. *Yanhai jingji kaifangqu jingji yanjiu he tongji ziliao [Economic Research and Statistical Materials on the Coastal Open Areas].* Beijing: Zhongguo tongji, 1989.

ZGFX80-87. Guojia tongji ju, nongcun shehui jingji tongji si [State Statistical Bureau, Rural Social and Economic Statistics Department]. *Zhongguo fenxian nongcun jingji tongji gaiyao 1980-1987 [Abstract of China's Rural Economic Statistics, by County, 1980-1987].* Beijing: Zhongguo tongji, 1989.

ZGFX88. Guojia tongji ju, nongcun shehui jingji tongji si. *Zhongguo fenxian nongcun jingji tongji gaiyao 1988.* Beijing: Zhongguo tongji, 1990.

ZGGYQY. Zhongguo gongye qiye quanji bianji weiyuanhui [Editorial Board of the Directory of China's Industrial Enterprises]. *Zhongguo gongye qiye quanji (fujian juan) [Directory of China's Industrial Enterprises (Fujian)].* Beijing: Zhongguo caizheng jingji, 1993.

ZGNYNJ91. Zhongguo nongye nianjian bianji weiyuanhui [Agricultural Yearbook of China Editorial Board]. *Zhongguo nongye nianjian 1991 [Agricultural Yearbook of China 1991].* Beijing: Nongye, 1991.

ZGQYGK. Zhongguo qiye gaikuang bianji weiyuanhui [China Enterprise Survey Editorial Board]. *Zhongguo qiye gaikuang [China Enterprise Survey],* v. 2. Beijing: Qiye guanli, 1988.

Zhang Ruiyao and Lu Zengrong. *Fujian diqu jingji [Fujian's Regional Economy].* Fuzhou: Fujian renmin, 1986.

Zhang Shoushan, Shao Jingfang, and Gao Jieguang. *Fujian duiwai jingmao sishi nian [Fujian's Foreign Economic Relations over Forty Years].* Fuzhou: Fujian ditu, 1989.

CORNELL EAST ASIA SERIES

No. 74 *Informal Empire in Crisis: British Diplomacy and the Chinese*
     Customs Succession, 1927-1929, by Martyn Atkins
Forthcoming: *The Gods Come Dancing: A Study of the Japanese Ritual*
     Dance of Yamabushi Kagura, by Irit Averbuch

For ordering information, please contact the Cornell East Asia Series,
East Asia Program, Cornell University, 140 Uris Hall, Ithaca, NY
14853-7601, USA; phone (607) 255-6222, fax (607) 255-1388.

8-94/.2M cloth/.5M paper/BB

www.ingramcontent.com/pod-product-compliance
Ingram Content Group UK Ltd.
Pitfield, Milton Keynes, MK11 3LW, UK
UKHW041914060225
454777UK00001B/317